W9-DCG-188

THE EASY 30-MINUTE COOKBOOK

The EASY 30-MINUTE COOKBOOK

100 FAST AND HEALTHY
Recipes for Busy People

Taylor Ellingson

Photography by Paul & Kimberley Sirisalee

ROCKRIDGE PRESS

Copyright © 2019 Rockridge Press, Emeryville, California

No part of this publication may be reproduced, stored in a retrieval system, or transmitted in any form or by any means, electronic, mechanical, photocopying, recording, scanning, or otherwise, except as permitted under Sections 107 or 108 of the 1976 United States Copyright Act, without the prior written permission of the Publisher. Requests to the Publisher for permission should be addressed to the Permissions Department, Rockridge Press, 6005 Shellmound Street, Suite 175, Emeryville, CA 94608.

Limit of Liability/Disclaimer of Warranty: The Publisher and the author make no representations or warranties with respect to the accuracy or completeness of the contents of this work and specifically disclaim all warranties, including without limitation warranties of fitness for a particular purpose. No warranty may be created or extended by sales or promotional materials. The advice and strategies contained herein may not be suitable for every situation. This work is sold with the understanding that the Publisher is not engaged in rendering medical, legal, or other professional advice or services. If professional assistance is required, the services of a competent professional person should be sought. Neither the Publisher nor the author shall be liable for damages arising herefrom. The fact that an individual, organization, or website is referred to in this work as a citation and/or potential source of further information does not mean that the author or the Publisher endorses the information the individual, organization, or website may provide or recommendations they/it may make. Further, readers should be aware that websites listed in this work may have changed or disappeared between when this work was written and when it is read.

For general information on our other products and services or to obtain technical support, please contact our Customer Care Department within the United States at (866) 744-2665, or outside the United States at (510) 253-0500.

Rockridge Press publishes its books in a variety of electronic and print formats. Some content that appears in print may not be available in electronic books, and vice versa.

TRADEMARKS: Rockridge Press and the Rockridge Press logo are trademarks or registered trademarks of Callisto Media Inc. and/or its affiliates, in the United States and other countries, and may not be used without written permission. All other trademarks are the property of their respective owners. Rockridge Press is not associated with any product or vendor mentioned in this book.

Interior and Cover Designer: Erin Yeung
Photo Art Director / Art Manager: Sue Bischoffberger
Editor: Rachel Feldman
Production Manager: Riley Hoffman
Production Editor: Kurt Shulenberger

Photography © 2019 Paul & Kimberley Sirisalee

ISBN: Print 978-1-64152-734-7 | eBook 978-1-64152-735-4

This book is dedicated to my husband, Marc, who has always been my favorite person to cook for, and our boys, Lars and Soren, whose ever-growing appetites make cooking even more fun.

Contents

Introduction

Listen, I get it. You're tired of takeout, tired of recipes that take forever, or just plain tired. Maybe you don't have an electric pressure cooker or don't like meal prepping, which can take up a whole day. Whatever the case, hi!—this cookbook is for you.

My interest in cooking began in graduate school when I lived alone in my first apartment with a full kitchen. I stuck to the basics for a couple of years but eventually got bored. I began making more creative dishes that were yummy and healthy, but still easy and quick to prepare, to maximize my minimal spare time. These days, with a husband and two small boys in tow, finding creative ways to get healthy, yummy dishes on the table as quickly as possible is my mission.

Food is important, but so is time. You shouldn't have to spend your entire night cooking—or your entire paycheck on eating out—to get a fast, tasty, healthy meal. The recipes in this book are cost-effective, healthy, delicious, and take only 30 minutes or less to make. And no, you don't have to be a savvy meal prepper or experienced home chef to make it work. This book makes it possible for anyone to make healthy, delicious food FAST.

My hope is that the recipes in this book give you back some of that precious time—to take your dog for a walk, help your kids with homework, or have some drinks with your friends. So, before you give up and go through the drive-thru—go through this book instead!

CHAPTER ONE
30 MINUTES TO THE TABLE

We can all use some shortcuts here and there, and luckily for us, there are tools and tricks that can make cooking easier and cut our time in the kitchen. In this chapter, I outline ways to become a more efficient cook, equipment that can make meal prep easier, ingredients to buy that are convenient but still healthy, and tips to outsmart your grocery store. This chapter is all about giving you the tools and tricks for stocking and working in the kitchen. That way, the next time you forget to plan ahead for dinner, you'll feel confident enough to make your OWN fast food.

Healthy Fast Food?

There are so many ways to get dinner on the table. Sure, you can make a dump-it-and-bake-it casserole, but it's probably going to take more than half an hour just to cook in the oven. You can throw together a grilled cheese sandwich and a bag of frozen veggies, but what's the fun in that? You can even make dinner from a box—say, something like beef stroganoff or chicken tetrazzini. But don't you dare look at the list of ingredients on the back of that package. Although the dish might not take a lot of brainpower to make, it's not the healthiest choice to power your brain.

So, yes, there are lots of ways cooking can be easy and fast, but this cookbook cares about what you're putting on your plate. The recipes in this cookbook are not only superfast and easy, but they're also made with ingredients that are *good* AND good for you. Say hello to fresh produce, fresh herbs, whole grains, and protein. Healthy food does not have to take a long time to prepare, and this cookbook is going to prove it.

Everyone has their own idea of healthy, but, in this cookbook, the recipes are made with fresh ingredients, include foods that have been minimally processed, and focus on a balance of good carbs, protein, and healthy fats. Most meals contain one serving of vegetables, and, if not, the recipe will refer you to my favorite side dish, quick Pan-Sautéed Vegetables (page 140). It is easy, healthy, and super adaptable to pairing with different cuisines! My Chickpea and Kale Curry (page 73) is a great example of a balanced meal: It has lots of fiber from chickpeas, nutrients from kale, and healthy fats from the coconut milk.

Finally, I encourage you to make your own decisions when it comes to your health. I've made specific substitution suggestions to make some dishes even healthier. But, in some cases, I encourage you to choose what you prefer, such as which grain to serve with your meal (whether it's rice or quinoa).

Cooking Hacks 101

If you've been thinking to yourself, "30 minutes or less? But *how*?!" this section is for you. These five hacks are all about using your tools wisely to keep time on your side in the kitchen. You'll be seeing hacks like these in the recipes throughout this book.

Don't wait for the preheat. If you're ready to put something in the oven but the oven's not quite preheated yet, just go ahead and put your dish in the oven. Once you get within 5 minutes of the recommended cooking time, start checking on the dish to determine readiness.

Get the water boiling immediately. Whenever you make something that requires boiling, such as making rice or pasta, start the water first. That is oftentimes the step that takes the longest, so it's important to get a jump-start on it.

Use the lid. When you sauté something in a skillet or a pan, put on a lid. Your dish will not only cook from the heat of the pan but will also steam from having the lid on, which will speed up your cooking time.

Maximize your microwave. Surprise—the microwave isn't just for frozen dinners and reheating leftovers. You can use the microwave to parcook vegetables to speed up the rest of the cooking time, like I did in my Taco Stuffed Peppers (page 131). Strategic microwaving can cut the cooking time for a recipe that would typically take 45 minutes down to just 15 minutes! Be sure to pick up some microwave-safe dishes (look for the telltale squiggly lines symbol on the bottom), ideally made out of glass.

Make the food processor your friend. Chopping vegetables can be one of the most time-consuming steps in a recipe, especially when you're not a seasoned cook. Using the food processor to chop onions, carrots, celery, and peppers—or any other diced vegetables that a recipe calls for—can save a ton of time. Invest in a small and a large one, if you can, and you will not regret it! Having both sizes is not necessary for the recipes in this cookbook, but it is convenient. If you must choose one, opt for the smaller one, which is easier to store and will be sufficient for the recipes included here.

Five Steps to Being a Fast Chef

Now that you know how to use your tools to be a faster cook, here's how you can use YOU to be faster. These five steps will help make you even more efficient in the kitchen.

1. **Be prepared.** *Read the entire recipe before you begin.* If you've ever started a recipe only to discover halfway through cooking that you don't have one of the key ingredients or tools . . . you know why this is important. Reading the recipe first also helps you get an overall sense of its steps, so you can just refer back when needed instead of stopping to read the directions. Being prepared also means getting out all the ingredients you need before starting to cook. In the restaurant industry, this is called *mise en place,* which is French for "everything in its place." When everything is out and ready, you don't have to waste time searching for ingredients while things are cooking.

2. **Have a compost/garbage bowl.** I keep a bowl on our counter for compost scraps. This way I don't have to constantly open the compost bin every time I have new scraps to toss in. When the food is cooking, I can work on cleaning up and putting the compost or garbage in the correct spot.

3. **Eyeball measurements.** The more you cook, the more you will be comfortable with this. I rarely measure salt and, unless I'm making a sauce or marinade, I typically eyeball measurements for things like dried spices.

4. **Always be multitasking.** There are pretty much always multiple things you can do at once while prepping a recipe. Whether it's heating a pan while you chop the vegetables or cleaning up while the food cooks, try to maximize your time by performing multiple steps at once.

5. **Cut food into smaller pieces.** It's basic science—smaller pieces of food cook faster! Smaller diced vegetables cook faster, thinly sliced chicken or steak will cook more quickly, and your overall dish will be done faster than if your food is cut into larger pieces.

Outsmart Your Supermarket

Follow these guidelines for smarter grocery shopping to make sure you're saving as much time and money as possible—and making the healthiest choices possible!

ALWAYS make a shopping list. This seems like a no-brainer, but I'm sure we can all relate to the situation of showing up at the grocery store hungry and without a plan. It never ends well! Write out a shopping list, organized by area of the store, and avoid aisles that you don't need anything from to decrease chances of impulse buying.

Read the labels—carefully! This will get easier with time, but when you are buying a new product or just getting to learn about something, read what's in it as well as the nutritional information. Compare other products for sodium level, sugar content, and the cleanest labels (i.e., the fewer the ingredients, the better!).

Buy generic brands. Most of the time, generic brands are the exact same thing as the name-brand versions—and cost much less. Be sure to compare labels to verify the generic brands have the same ingredients and don't contain more sugar or sodium.

Avoid busy times. If you can, avoid the grocery store on the weekends and, instead, grocery shop on a weekday morning or evening, when there are typically fewer people shopping. If getting to the store on a weekday is too difficult, try to go first thing on a Saturday or Sunday morning before it gets too busy. This will save you time, as you won't have to dodge carts and wait for others in line. It will also help you feel less rushed, giving you time to read labels, look for sales, and make smart decisions.

Use a list app on your phone. I use an app on my phone not only to make my grocery list but also to keep track of other reminders, including the Dirty Dozen™ and the Clean Fifteen™ (see page 146—take a pic!), what seafood is the most sustainable, and what product brands I like best and have the most nutritional value. That way, I can easily bring up this information when I'm out shopping and don't have to waste time googling or guessing!

The Convenient Kitchen

Ever watch an infomercial? There are hundreds (thousands?!) of different kitchen appliances out there promising to make our lives easier. I've lived in a number of places with fairly limited storage space in the kitchen, so I am very selective about which appliances and gadgets get a spot in my cabinets. Following you will find the kitchen equipment I find absolutely essential, gadgets that will make your life easier when it comes to cooking and are completely worth the kitchen space, and ingredients I always have on hand that will make cooking easier and more convenient.

Essential Equipment

These are my trusty, go-to pieces of equipment when preparing fast and easy dishes. I highly recommend investing in all of these items if you don't have them in your kitchen already!

Baking sheet. Baking sheets aren't only for cookies—they are great for one-pan meals. I like to have one designated specifically for roasting vegetables (a rimmed version helps keep my food on the sheet!) and making one-pan meals, as pans used for roasting tend to get worn and a little more seasoned faster than the ones I use solely for baking.

Blender/immersion blender. A high-speed blender is a great investment for those who not only make smoothies regularly but also enjoy soups and sauces. High-speed blenders are also great for making nut flours and nut milk, and even to grind spices.

Pots (2). Have a small-to-medium pot for things like cooking rice or grains, and a large one for soups.

Skillets (2). Skillets are crucial for dishes like stir-fries, sautéed vegetables, and pan-seared meat. It's helpful to have one large skillet and one medium skillet to use when preparing different amounts of food.

Wooden spoon. A trusty wooden spoon can be used for stirring anything and everything—from vegetables and soups to oatmeal and cookie dough.

Shelf Life: Did You Know?

It's always a bummer to open up a produce drawer to find limp celery and herbs past their prime. Fresh produce is not cheap—so why do we waste it? There are a few tricks to storing produce that will help your herbs and vegetables stay fresher longer. You'll feel good knowing that food won't go to waste quickly, you'll use more fresh produce, and you'll save time and money by avoiding additional purchases!

1. Freeze fresh ginger to preserve its freshness longer, as well as make it easier to mince.

2. Have an extra half an onion? Dice it and freeze it—it will be ready to use the next time you need one.

3. Store your herbs in a Mason jar with water, like a bouquet of flowers for your fridge. It will help keep them fresher longer.

4. Store fresh greens with a paper towel in a sealed plastic bag to prevent the greens from wilting or getting slimy.

5. Keep the fruit and vegetable drawers as dry as possible. Any moisture will speed up spoiling. Remove any rotten or very ripe produce immediately as well, to avoid encouraging other produce to ripen faster.

6. Store mushrooms in a paper bag in the refrigerator and keep them as dry as possible.

7. Keep bananas away from other vegetables you want to keep fresh. Bananas emit the highest levels of ethylene gas of any fruit or vegetable, which encourages ripening of produce.

8. Avoid washing berries until you use them, as the moisture will encourage them to degrade.

9. Store tomatoes at room temperature and away from sunlight, as the sun will ripen and spoil them.

10. Different versions of the same ingredient can last longer. Organic milk lasts longer than regular milk; white rice lasts longer than brown rice.

Gadgets for People Who Hate Food Prep

There are thousands of weird gadgets out there—hot dog slicers, egg cubers, strawberry stem removers—I mean, really! But there are a few special tools I would recommend to make food prep (and thus life in general) a lot easier.

Garlic press. I really dislike mincing fresh garlic with a knife because my fingers smell like garlic for hours. The garlic press takes a fraction of the time—and, bonus: no stinky garlic fingers!

Mini food processor. If I'm just not in the mood to do a lot of vegetable chopping, I break out my mini food processor. It does a great (and fast!) job at dicing vegetables such as onions, bell peppers, carrots, celery, and even herbs. If you're on a budget, an onion chopper will also do the trick; it just involves a little more hands-on work.

Rice cooker. We cook a lot of rice and grains in our house, and they are suggested in many of the recipes in this cookbook. Using a rice cooker takes away the need to watch it while you prepare the rest of the meal, freeing up time for cooking. Many times, an electric pressure cooker has a rice cooking option, so if you have one of those be sure to use it!

Sharp knife. There's nothing more frustrating than trying to chop veggies or meat with a dull knife. It takes longer and is actually quite dangerous. A well-sharpened knife ensures clean cuts and no slippage because it's dull!

Zester. Although a zester is traditionally used for zesting citrus, I use mine all the time for grating fresh ginger. You'll notice I use fresh ginger in my recipes a lot, so having a zester to speed up the process of mincing ginger is very handy!

Time-Saving Ingredients

Having a few key staples on hand will not only reduce the time you're spending at the grocery store every week, but it will also make deciding what to cook for dinner a lot easier. No more excuses for not making a dish because you don't have a key ingredient!

PANTRY

Canned beans. Canned beans are such an easy and quick source of protein and are a great ingredient for easy meals. Unlike their dried counterpart, canned beans don't require hours of soaking or cooking, and still taste great.

Coconut milk. I always have a can or two of coconut milk in our pantry to use for smoothies, soups, and curries, which we often cook. Coconut milk also makes a great substitute for milk if you want to make a dish dairy-free.

Grains. I always have a variety of grains on hand, including quinoa, farro, couscous, wheat berries, and quick-cooking barley, all of which, generally, have the same purpose but different timeframes for cooking. If I'm short on time, I reach for couscous or quick-cooking barley, but if I have some extra time, I love the extra fiber I get from brown rice and wheat berries, and the protein from quinoa. I also always have a couple of packets of microwavable brown rice on hand, which take 90 seconds to cook and are just so easy when I'm really in a pinch!

Marinara. It isn't just for spaghetti! Jarred marinara is so versatile and, because it is already seasoned—usually with Italian spices and garlic—it doesn't need a lot more added to it for flavor.

Spice blends. Having spice blends on hand—whether store-bought or homemade— saves you time in the kitchen, as you won't have to measure out every single spice that is in the blend individually. Try Cajun seasoning, Curry Powder (page 135), Italian seasoning, or Taco Seasoning Mix (page 136).

FRIDGE

Eggs. Eggs have a long shelf life and are a great source of protein at any meal. They are also easy and fast to prepare in many different ways!

Jarred minced garlic. Although I love using fresh garlic, I also love taking advantage of jarred minced garlic because of its ease and great flavor. Jarred garlic is easily stored in my refrigerator door and means I have one less kitchen gadget to clean!

Plain Greek yogurt. Having Greek yogurt on hand is great because it can be used in so many ways: added to smoothies for an extra protein boost, used in baking or in place of sour cream, and, of course, as the base for breakfast or a snack, topped with fruit and granola.

Shredded cheese. Buying shredded cheese saves you the time and trouble of not only shredding cheese but also cleaning the grater. The cheese grater is one of my all-time least favorite utensils to clean, so I am a huge fan of bagged shredded cheese!

Tube of minced ginger. I cook a lot with fresh ginger, using it in my curries and Thai food. Just as with jarred garlic, having a tube of minced ginger in the refrigerator helps save time when I really need to get dinner on the table fast and am looking to cut corners any chance I get.

FREEZER

Bread. Bread is so versatile. Its obvious use is for sandwiches, but I also use bread to make breakfast casseroles, bread crumbs, and French toast.

Frozen vegetables. Frozen vegetables that are packaged without any oil or spices have the same health benefits as fresh vegetables. In fact, when you have the choice between canned or frozen—always go frozen! These vegetables (and fruits) are frozen at their peak ripeness and don't have any added sodium or sugar as canned vegetables and fruits do. Frozen fruits and vegetables are also often already chopped, saving prep time.

Meat and seafood. I prefer starting my recipes with meat that has been thawed in the refrigerator, as it cooks faster, but it is also nice to have a well-stocked freezer of meat options. Having frozen meat and seafood on hand is better than nothing, and it will prevent last-minute decisions to grab takeout or just have a bowl of cereal for dinner. My go-tos are shrimp, chicken breast, and ground beef.

Tortillas. Having tortillas on hand will save you in so many ways. Whether you use them to eat your eggs and bacon on the go in a breakfast taco, make a turkey wrap for lunch, or whip up vegetarian enchiladas for dinner, tortillas can be used at every meal.

Making Cleanup Easy

Sure, it may only take 30 minutes to make the meal, but if it takes an hour afterward to clean up, doesn't that defeat the whole purpose of saving time?

Use parchment paper or aluminum foil. Line the baking sheet or pan with parchment paper or aluminum foil to cut down on the amount of cleaning.

Soak while you eat. Soak dishes that you will wash by hand while you eat so they are ready to be cleaned when you are finished.

Start with an empty dishwasher and a clean sink. Having your dishwasher empty will make it easier and faster to load while you are cleaning up, and a clean, empty sink is ready for dishes to be hand-washed immediately.

Have a garbage bowl. Having a garbage bowl handy reduces the number of times you have to access the garbage can and keeps the countertop clear of clutter.

Measure dry ingredients first, if possible. This way, you can use the same measuring spoons and cups for the wet ingredients.

About the Recipes

You probably know by now that the recipes in this book take only 30 minutes or less to prep and cook, but here are some ways we're making it even easier for you.

Labels that indicate that a recipe is even easier. You'll see the following labels on recipes and the table of contents for every chapter:

- Superfast (dishes that take only 10 minutes)
- One Pot (using only 1 main piece of equipment)
- 5-Ingredient (not including salt, pepper, and oil)
- No Cook (no cooking required)

Tips for every situation. You'll see the following tips throughout this book:

Love Your Leftovers: How to use leftover ingredients to reduce waste

Make It Easier: How to reduce steps or cut down on prep time

Make It Faster: How to make a recipe even faster by using a premade/prechopped version of an ingredient

Make It Healthier: How to make a recipe even healthier by swapping one ingredient for another

Make It Yourself: How to use a homemade ingredient instead of a store-bought one

Serving Tip: Suggestions for sides or variations to make a complete meal

Simple Swap: Tips for using what's on hand if you don't have an ingredient

Smart Shopping: Advice for buying healthier and more affordable premade items

A chapter with optional make-them-yourself staples. Occasionally a recipe will call for a store-bought item made with unprocessed ingredients to make your life easier (i.e., jarred pesto or teriyaki sauce). If you have a bit more time and want to make the item yourself, however, you can refer to the recipes in chapter 9.

CHAPTER TWO

BREAKFAST

Breakfast is an often-forgotten meal of the day, replaced with coffee and a granola bar or skipped altogether. I am a firm believer that a good day starts with a great breakfast, and it does not have to take a lot of time! Whether you have 10 minutes to make a Strawberry Cauliflower Smoothie (page 15), or want something warm to wrap your hands around, like Bacon Cheddar Breakfast Tacos (page 20), your day will be better because of it.

STRAWBERRY CAULIFLOWER SMOOTHIE

SERVES: 2 to 3 | **PREP TIME:** 5 minutes |

Did I lose you at cauliflower? I promise—you can't taste it! I started adding cauliflower to all of my smoothies a couple years ago and have never looked back. Cauliflower adds a dose of nutrients (vitamins C, K, and B6), fiber, and antioxidants, and you really can't taste it. This strawberry smoothie gets an even bigger health boost from the ground flaxseed and chia seeds, which are optional but always make me feel like I'm getting the most out of my smoothies.

4 cups unsweetened vanilla almond milk

2 cups frozen strawberries

1 frozen banana

1 cup frozen cauliflower

2 tablespoons honey

2 tablespoons ground flaxseed (optional)

1 tablespoon chia seeds (optional)

Prepare the smoothie. In a high-speed blender, combine the milk, strawberries, banana, cauliflower, honey, flaxseed (if using), and chia seeds (if using). Blend on high speed until smooth and creamy.

Simple Swap: Feel free to use fresh strawberries and bananas, and add ½ cup of ice. This recipe is best with frozen cauliflower, as it adds a creaminess to the consistency.

Per Serving: Calories: 259; Saturated Fat: 0g; Total Fat: 6g; Protein: 4g; Total Carbs: 50g; Fiber: 8g; Sodium: 376mg

FRUIT AND YOGURT BREAKFAST WRAPS

SERVES: 4 | **PREP TIME:** 10 minutes | 🕐

I first started making fruit and yogurt wraps for my kids, but they have quickly become a family favorite. They're healthy, filling, and delicious! They're also very adaptable to different taste preferences. Use your favorite nut butter and whatever fruit you have on hand. My family also loves using chocolate-hazelnut spread (like Nutella) for a fun dessert treat.

1 cup plain whole-milk Greek yogurt

2 tablespoons honey

2 tablespoons nut butter of choice

4 whole-wheat taco-size tortillas

1 banana, sliced

½ cup chopped fresh strawberries

½ cup fresh blueberries

1. **Prepare the yogurt mix.** In a small bowl, stir together the yogurt, honey, and nut butter.

2. **Prepare the tortillas.** Spread ¼ cup of the yogurt mixture onto each tortilla, leaving about ½ inch of space around the edge so it does not spill out once wrapped.

3. **Finish.** Evenly divide the fruit on top of the yogurt and roll the tortillas into wraps.

Make It Healthier: I prefer using whole-milk yogurt because I find it more satisfying, but you can use low-fat yogurt if you prefer.

Per Serving: Calories: 299; Saturated Fat: 3g; Total Fat: 9g; Protein: 11g; Total Carbs: 47g; Fiber: 4g; Sodium: 249mg

TROPICAL SMOOTHIE BOWLS

SERVES: 4 | **PREP TIME:** 10 minutes |

Smoothie bowls are a great way to make a smoothie into more of a meal. They are made with less liquid, creating a thicker texture that is best eaten with a spoon—and topped with all sorts of delicious, healthy ingredients. I like topping my smoothie bowls with a combination of chia seeds, coconut, fruit, and nuts for some chewy and some crunchy!

1½ cups unsweetened
   vanilla coconut milk
2 cups frozen pineapple
2 cups frozen mango
2 frozen bananas
2 tablespoons honey
2 tablespoons chia seeds
½ cup shredded coconut
½ cup chopped cashews
2 kiwis, peeled
   and chopped

1. **Blend the ingredients.** In a high-speed blender, combine the coconut milk, pineapple, mango, bananas, and honey. Blend on high speed until smooth. The mixture will be quite thick.

2. **Finish.** Divide the mixture among 4 bowls and top each with chia seeds, coconut, cashews, and kiwi. Serve and enjoy.

Make It Faster: You can often find a bag of frozen mixed tropical fruit at the grocery store, which would reduce the time it takes to measure the different fruits. Just use about 6 cups tropical fruit mix instead of the pineapple, mango, and banana.

Simple Swap: Frozen fruit works best in this recipe, but if you want to substitute fresh fruit, be sure to add 1½ cups of ice to get the correct frozen consistency.

Per Serving: Calories: 411; Saturated Fat: 9g; Total Fat: 19g; Protein: 6g; Total Carbs: 62g; Fiber: 10g; Sodium: 11mg

PEANUT BUTTER AND JELLY YOGURT PARFAITS

SERVES: 4 | **PREP TIME:** 10 minutes | 🕐

Some mornings (okay, MOST mornings) a bowl of yogurt just isn't going to cut it for me. I need some substance to my breakfasts! These yogurt parfaits are packed with protein from the Greek yogurt and peanut butter, which will keep you going until lunchtime. I like strawberry for the nostalgic PB & J flavor, but feel free to use whatever berries you like best.

½ cup peanut butter

2 tablespoons honey

4 cups plain whole-milk Greek yogurt

4 tablespoons strawberry jam

1 cup granola

1 cup chopped fresh strawberries

1. **Prepare the peanut butter.** In a small microwave-safe bowl, combine the peanut butter and honey. Microwave on high power for 20 seconds. Stir to combine and microwave for 10 seconds more.

2. **Assemble the yogurt bowls.** Add ½ cup of the yogurt to each of 4 bowls or parfait cups. Drizzle 1 tablespoon of the peanut butter mixture and 1 tablespoon of jam over each. Sprinkle over each 1 tablespoon of the granola and 1 tablespoon of the strawberries.

3. **Finish.** Divide the remaining yogurt among the bowls and drizzle with the remaining peanut butter. Sprinkle on the remaining granola and top with the remaining strawberries.

Make It Faster: You can use strawberry Greek yogurt instead of plain Greek yogurt and omit the strawberry jam to reduce the number of ingredients and steps needed for this recipe.

Per Serving: Calories: 569; Saturated Fat: 13g; Total Fat: 41g; Protein: 35g; Total Carbs: 77g; Fiber: 8g; Sodium: 234mg

ZUCCHINI AND TOMATO AVOCADO TOAST

SERVES: 4 | **PREP TIME:** 10 minutes **COOK TIME:** 9 minutes

Avocado toast might have started as a trendy food, but I don't see it going away any time soon! Avocado toast offers a great combination of fat, protein, and carbs, and it can be jazzed up in so many ways. In this recipe, I utilize summer veggies and herbs for maximum flavor and nutrition, making this toast a good meal for breakfast, brunch, or lunchtime.

1 tablespoon olive oil

2 zucchini, sliced lengthwise and cut into thin bite-size pieces

1 cup cherry tomatoes, halved

2 garlic cloves, minced

½ teaspoon salt

4 slices bread

2 avocados, peeled and pitted

¼ cup chopped fresh basil

1. **Cook the zucchini and cherry tomatoes.** In a large skillet over medium-high heat, heat the oil. Add the zucchini and cherry tomatoes and cook for about 8 minutes, or until softened. Add the garlic and salt and cook for 1 minute more.

2. **Prepare the bread and avocado.** While the zucchini and tomatoes cook, toast the bread and mash the avocados with the back of a fork in a small bowl.

3. **Finish.** Spread ¼ of the avocado on each piece of toast. Top with the zucchini and tomato mixture and sprinkle each with 1 tablespoon of the basil.

Per Serving: Calories: 270; Saturated Fat: 3g; Total Fat: 18g; Protein: 7g; Total Carbs: 25g; Fiber: 10g; Sodium: 442mg

BACON CHEDDAR BREAKFAST TACOS

SERVES: 4 | **PREP TIME:** 10 minutes **COOK TIME:** 15 minutes

Tacos for breakfast? Yes, please! These tacos are warm tortillas filled with fluffy scrambled eggs, smoky bacon, and shredded cheese. We love topping our breakfast tacos with salsa and avocado for more flavor and some healthy fat.

8 bacon slices

8 large eggs

2 tablespoons milk

1 tablespoon butter

½ cup shredded Cheddar cheese, divided

1 scallion, chopped

8 taco-size tortillas

Salsa, for topping

1 avocado, peeled, pitted, and diced, for topping

1. **Cook the bacon.** Place the bacon in a cold skillet and place the skillet over medium heat. Cook the bacon for 8 to 12 minutes, or to your desired crispiness. Transfer the bacon to paper towels to drain.

2. **Prepare the eggs.** While the bacon cooks, in a medium bowl, whisk the eggs and milk until blended.

3. **Cook the eggs.** In a medium skillet over medium-low heat, melt the butter. Scramble the egg mixture, cooking for about 5 minutes and stirring frequently with a heat-proof spatula, about every 30 seconds. Stir in ¼ cup of the cheese and the scallion. Cook for 1 minute more, or until the cheese melts.

4. **Crumble the bacon.** Crumble the cooked bacon into bite-size pieces and set aside.

5. **Heat the tortillas.** Place the tortillas on a plate and cover them with a damp paper towel. Microwave the tortillas on high power for 30 to 60 seconds, until warm.

6. **Finish.** Divide the scrambled eggs among the tortillas. Top each with the bacon, the remaining ¼ cup of cheese, salsa, and diced avocado.

Make It Faster: Cook the bacon in bulk ahead of time or buy precooked bacon at the grocery store to reduce the cooking time and prep work.

Per Serving: Calories: 661; Saturated Fat: 14g; Total Fat: 44g; Protein: 48g; Total Carbs: 18g; Fiber: 13g; Sodium: 1,765mg

ROASTED RED PEPPER AND GOAT CHEESE EGG MUFFINS

SERVES: 4 to 6 | **PREP TIME:** 10 minutes **COOK TIME:** 18 minutes |

Egg muffins are the perfect way to eat eggs on the go. These vegetarian egg muffins are a great source of protein and are packed with flavor from the roasted red peppers and goat cheese. The muffins are a breeze to whip up in the morning, but they are also great to make in advance and microwave on extra-busy days.

Nonstick cooking spray
10 large eggs
1 cup milk
1 teaspoon salt
½ teaspoon pepper
½ cup diced jarred roasted red peppers, drained
1 cup chopped fresh baby spinach leaves
½ cup crumbled goat cheese

1. **Preheat the oven and prepare the muffin pan.** Preheat the oven to 400°F. Coat 12 cups of a muffin pan with cooking spray. Set aside.

2. **Prepare the egg mixture.** In a large bowl, whisk the eggs, milk, salt, and pepper until blended.

3. **Add the vegetables.** Divide the red peppers and spinach among the prepared muffin cups.

4. **Add the egg mixture.** Divide the egg mixture among the muffin cups. Sprinkle each with 2 teaspoons of goat cheese.

5. **Finish.** Bake for 15 to 18 minutes, or until the muffins are golden brown and set.

Make It Yourself: If you have time, make your own Roasted Red Peppers (page 141).

Per Serving: Calories: 270; Saturated Fat: 6g; Total Fat: 16g; Protein: 20g; Total Carbs: 7g; Fiber: 0g; Sodium: 984mg

MIXED BERRY PANCAKE MUFFINS

SERVES: 4 to 6 | **PREP TIME:** 10 minutes **COOK TIME:** 15 minutes

Pancake mix isn't just for pancakes! Using pancake mix for muffins helps reduce the time it takes to measure all the different ingredients that go into muffins—and they turn out super fluffy and perfect every time. We usually just throw in whatever berries we have in the refrigerator—and voilà!

Nonstick cooking spray
2 cups store-bought pancake mix
⅓ cup sugar
1 large egg
⅔ cup milk
3 tablespoons butter, melted
1½ cups mixed fresh berries, such as raspberries, blueberries, and strawberries

1. **Preheat the oven and prepare the muffin pan.** Preheat the oven to 400°F. Coat 10 cups of a muffin pan with cooking spray. Set aside.

2. **Prepare the batter.** In a large bowl, stir together the pancake mix, sugar, egg, milk, and butter until just combined. Fold in the berries. Divide the batter among the prepared muffin cups, filling each about ¾ full.

3. **Finish.** Bake for 15 minutes, or until the muffins are slightly golden and a toothpick inserted into the center comes out clean.

Smart Shopping: I use Kodiak Cakes pancake mix because it's full of whole-grain wheat and oat flours.

Make It Yourself: If you have time, make your own Pancake Mix (page 139) from scratch.

Per Serving: Calories: 365; Saturated Fat: 13g; Total Fat: 7g; Protein: 8g; Total Carbs: 59g; Fiber: 12g; Sodium: 365mg

CHORIZO BAKED EGGS

SERVES: 2 to 4 | PREP TIME: 10 minutes COOK TIME: 20 minutes |

Chorizo is why I can't be a vegetarian. It's my all-time favorite meat because it has so much flavor! The scallion and cilantro add fresh flavor to this dish and the Cotija cheese complements the spiciness from the chorizo.

1 tablespoon olive oil

1 pound ground chorizo

1 small onion, diced

1 (28-ounce) can tomato sauce

4 large eggs

¾ cup Cotija cheese

1 avocado, peeled, pitted, and diced

¼ cup chopped scallions

¼ cup chopped fresh cilantro

Bread or tortillas, toasted or warmed, for serving

1. **Cook the chorizo.** In a medium cast iron skillet over medium-high heat, heat the oil. Add the ground chorizo and onion and cook for 5 to 7 minutes, or until the chorizo is cooked through and the onion is softened. Stir in the tomato sauce.

2. **Add the eggs.** With the back of a large spoon, make four wells in the mixture. Crack one egg into each well.

3. **Cook the eggs.** Cover the skillet and cook for 5 to 10 minutes, or until the whites are set and the yolk is at your preferred doneness. I like cooking the eggs for 5 minutes, or until the whites are cooked and the yolk is still runny. If you prefer a firmer yolk, cook for 8 to 10 minutes.

4. **Finish.** Serve the eggs and chorizo mixture topped with the cheese, avocado, scallion, and cilantro. It's especially tasty with a slice of buttered sourdough toast or some warm tortillas.

Smart Shopping: Look for chorizo that is not in casings so you don't have to spend time removing the meat from the casings.

Per Serving: Calories: 1,043; Saturated Fat: 21g; Total Fat: 66g; Protein: 74g; Total Carbs: 49g; Fiber: 17g; Sodium: 4,187mg

ONE-SKILLET BISCUITS AND SAUSAGE GRAVY

SERVES: 4 to 6 | **PREP TIME:** 5 minutes **COOK TIME:** 25 minutes |

I'm not sure how biscuits and gravy ever became a breakfast item, but I am here for it. I mean, how do you go wrong with creamy sausage gravy and fluffy buttermilk biscuits? This recipe is deceptively easy and, with the help of canned biscuits, can be on your table in 30 minutes!

1 pound breakfast sausage
2 tablespoons butter
¼ cup all-purpose flour
3 cups milk
½ teaspoon salt
½ teaspoon freshly ground
  black pepper
1 (16-ounce) can buttermilk
  biscuits, separated and
  quartered

1. **Preheat the oven.** Preheat the oven to 400°F.

2. **Cook the sausage.** Heat a large cast iron skillet over medium-high heat. Add the sausage to the hot skillet and cook for 8 to 10 minutes, breaking it apart with the back of a wooden spoon as it cooks, until it is no longer pink.

3. **Prepare the gravy.** Add the butter to the sausage and stir until melted and combined. Add the flour, stirring well to combine, and cook for 30 seconds. Slowly pour in the milk, whisking to combine and create a gravy. Season with the salt and pepper and cook for 1 to 2 minutes more, until the gravy thickens and coats the back of a spoon.

4. **Add the biscuits.** Place the biscuit pieces on top of the sausage gravy.

5. **Finish.** Bake for 12 to 14 minutes, or until the biscuits are slightly golden and cooked through.

Smart Shopping: I like to use Annie's refrigerated biscuits in this recipe, as they are made with wheat flour and fewer ingredients than other brands.

Per Serving: Calories: 876; Saturated Fat: 22g; Total Fat: 55g; Protein: 32g; Total Carbs: 63g; Fiber: 2g; Sodium: 2,135mg

LEMON CHEESECAKE-STUFFED FRENCH TOAST

SERVES: 4 | **PREP TIME:** 10 minutes **COOK TIME:** 12 minutes

Cheesecake-stuffed French toast is one of my go-to weekend breakfasts. First, it's EASY. Second, my kids love it. This lemon variation is so springy and full of flavor that you don't even need syrup! Just a dusting of powdered sugar and breakfast is served.

For the filling

8 ounces cream cheese, at room temperature
2 teaspoons freshly squeezed lemon juice
2 teaspoons lemon zest
2 teaspoons sugar

For the batter

¾ cup milk
4 large eggs
1 tablespoon sugar

For cooking and serving

8 slices bread
4 tablespoons butter
Powdered sugar, for serving

1. **Preheat the griddle.** Preheat a griddle over medium-high heat.

2. **Prepare the filling.** In a medium bowl, combine the cream cheese, lemon juice, lemon zest, and sugar. Using either a handheld electric mixer or a fork, mix well.

3. **Prepare the batter.** In a shallow bowl, whisk the milk, eggs, and sugar until well blended.

4. **Prepare the bread.** Place 4 slices of the bread on a work surface and slather each with ¼ of the cream cheese mixture. Top with the remaining 4 slices of bread.

5. **Cook the toasts.** Melt the butter on the hot griddle. One at a time, dip each stuffed sandwich into the batter, turning to coat both sides. Let any excess batter drip off and immediately place the sandwich on the hot griddle. Cook for 3 to 4 minutes per side, or until golden brown.

6. **Finish.** Serve sprinkled with powdered sugar.

Per Serving: Calories: 466; Saturated Fat: 22g; Total Fat: 38g; Protein: 14g; Total Carbs: 20g; Fiber: 1g; Sodium: 464mg

GUACAMOLE BREAKFAST SANDWICHES

SERVES: 4 | **PREP TIME:** 12 minutes **COOK TIME:** 15 minutes

No need to pay extra for premade guacamole at a supermarket. Just make it at home and slather it on your breakfast sandwich! I love using a thick sourdough bread for these sandwiches because it complements all the goodness that lies between the slices really well.

8 bacon slices

2 avocados, peeled and pitted

¼ red onion, diced

Juice of 1 lime

2 tablespoons chopped fresh cilantro

¼ teaspoon salt

2 tablespoons olive oil

4 large eggs

8 slices bread

1. **Cook the bacon.** Place the bacon in a cold skillet and place the skillet over medium heat. Cook the bacon for 8 to 12 minutes, or to your desired crispiness. Transfer the bacon to paper towels to drain.

2. **Prepare the guacamole.** While the bacon cooks, mash the avocado with the back of a fork in a medium bowl. Stir in the onion, lime juice, cilantro, and salt. Set aside.

3. **Cook the eggs.** In a nonstick skillet over medium-high heat, heat the oil. Crack the eggs into the skillet and cook over easy for 2 to 3 minutes per side, until the yolk reaches your desired doneness.

4. **Toast the bread.** While the eggs cook, toast the bread.

5. **Assemble the sandwiches.** Place 4 pieces of toast on a work surface and spread each with ¼ of the guacamole. Top each piece with 1 egg and 2 bacon slices.

6. **Finish.** Top with the remaining 4 slices of toast and serve.

Per Serving: Calories: 535; Saturated Fat: 42g; Total Fat: 10g; Protein: 24g; Total Carbs: 19g; Fiber: 7g; Sodium: 1,225mg

CHAPTER THREE
SALADS AND SOUPS

We all know we should eat more vegetables, and I'm here to tell you that they can actually be delicious! These soup and salad recipes will have you not only tolerating vegetables but also craving them. Your friends will beg you to make my Blueberry Caprese (page 31) for every barbecue, and you won't believe how easy and delicious the Roasted Red Pepper Gazpacho (page 38) is. And just you wait until there's a chill in the air—you will be craving Creamy White Chicken Lasagna Soup (page 42).

BLUEBERRY CAPRESE

SERVES: 4 | PREP TIME: 10 minutes | 🚫 🕐

No other salad screams "SUMMER!" to me like caprese salad does. We usually hit up the farmers' market in the warmer months for fresh tomatoes and basil. I also added fresh blueberries for a pop of flavor and color—they add a perfect summery twist!

For the salad

2 cups cherry tomatoes

1 cup fresh blueberries

8 ounces fresh
mozzarella balls

¼ cup chopped fresh basil

For the dressing

2 tablespoons olive oil

1 tablespoon white
balsamic vinegar

¼ teaspoon salt

¼ teaspoon freshly ground
black pepper

1. **Prepare the salad base.** In a large bowl, combine the tomatoes, blueberries, mozzarella, and basil. Set aside.

2. **Prepare the dressing.** In a small bowl, whisk the oil, vinegar, salt, and pepper until combined.

3. **Finish.** Pour the dressing over the salad and toss to combine.

Per Serving: Calories: 260; Saturated Fat: 8g; Total Fat: 19g; Protein: 15g; Total Carbs: 9g; Fiber: 2g; Sodium: 246mg

TUSCAN BEAN AND ARUGULA SALAD

SERVES: 4 | PREP TIME: 15 minutes |

If you're looking for a seemingly fancy salad to take to a dinner party, but don't want to put in a ton of work, look no further. This salad is bursting with different flavors and textures and really could not be easier. This dish is sure to be a crowd-pleaser, perfect for a light lunch or dinner with some crusty bread on the side.

For the dressing

⅓ cup olive oil

2 tablespoons balsamic vinegar

2 garlic cloves, minced

1 teaspoon Italian seasoning

½ teaspoon salt

½ teaspoon freshly ground black pepper

For the salad

2 (16-ounce) cans cannellini beans, rinsed and drained

1 small red onion, diced

1 cup diced jarred roasted red peppers, drained

1 (6-ounce) jar marinated artichoke hearts, drained

¼ cup chopped fresh basil

2 cups fresh arugula

½ cup shredded Parmesan cheese

1. **Prepare the dressing.** In a small bowl, whisk the oil, vinegar, garlic, Italian seasoning, salt, and pepper until combined. Set aside.

2. **Prepare the salad base.** In a large bowl, combine the beans, onion, red peppers, artichoke hearts, basil, and arugula.

3. **Finish.** Pour the dressing over the bean mixture and gently stir to coat. Top with the Parmesan cheese.

Make It Yourself: If you have extra time, make your own Roasted Red Peppers (page 141).

Per Serving: Calories: 479; Saturated Fat: 6g; Total Fat: 27g; Protein: 17g; Total Carbs: 43g; Fiber: 13g; Sodium: 1,140mg

STRAWBERRY AVOCADO SALAD

SERVES: 4 | **PREP TIME:** 15 minutes |

I've been making this strawberry salad for years, and I always get comments about how good it is. My secret? Putting a few strawberries in the dressing! They get blended in with other simple ingredients such as olive oil and balsamic vinegar and add just the right amount of sweetness and extra fruit flavor.

For the dressing

3 whole strawberries, hulled

¼ cup olive oil

2 tablespoons balsamic vinegar

1 garlic clove, peeled

¼ teaspoon salt

¼ teaspoon freshly ground black pepper

For the salad

6 cups fresh baby spinach leaves

2 cups sliced strawberries

½ red onion, thinly sliced

1 avocado, peeled, pitted, and diced

½ cup crumbled feta cheese

¼ cup sliced almonds

1. **Prepare the dressing.** In a food processor, combine the whole strawberries, oil, vinegar, garlic, salt, and pepper. Blend until smooth. Set aside.

2. **Prepare the salad base.** In a large bowl, combine the spinach, sliced strawberries, and onion.

3. **Finish.** Drizzle the salad base with the dressing and toss to combine. Top with the avocado, feta cheese and almonds.

Per Serving: Calories: 310; Saturated Fat: 6g; Total Fat: 27g; Protein: 7g; Total Carbs: 16g; Fiber: 7g; Sodium: 398mg

CRANBERRY PECAN TORTELLINI SALAD

SERVES: 4 to 6 | **PREP TIME:** 10 minutes **COOK TIME:** 7 minutes

This is half leafy salad and half pasta salad, which really is the best of both worlds, right? It's also sweet and savory and full of different textures—from crunchy romaine lettuce and chopped pecans to chewy tortellini and cranberries. There's something for everybody in this salad!

For the salad

2 cups (9 ounces) frozen cheese tortellini

1 head romaine lettuce, chopped (about 4 cups)

½ cup crumbled feta cheese

⅓ cup dried cranberries

¼ cup chopped pecans

For the dressing

⅓ cup olive oil

3 tablespoons balsamic vinegar

1 teaspoon sugar

1 teaspoon minced garlic

½ teaspoon salt

¼ teaspoon freshly ground black pepper

1. **Cook the pasta.** Bring a large pot of water to a boil over high heat. Add the tortellini and cook according to the package directions. Drain the cooked tortellini and rinse with cold water.

2. **Prepare the salad base.** In a large bowl, combine the lettuce, cooked tortellini, feta cheese, cranberries, and pecans.

3. **Prepare the dressing.** While the pasta cooks, in a small bowl, whisk the oil, vinegar, sugar, garlic, salt, and pepper until combined. Set aside.

4. **Finish.** Add the dressing to the salad and toss well to combine.

Smart Shopping: Use bagged romaine lettuce to reduce prep time. You can also use a good-quality balsamic vinaigrette, such as Litehouse, instead of making your own to cut down on prep.

Per Serving: Calories: 424; Saturated Fat: 8g; Total Fat: 30g; Protein: 10g; Total Carbs: 32g; Fiber: 2g; Sodium: 690mg

GRILLED PEACH PANZANELLA SALAD

SERVES: 4 to 6 | **PREP TIME:** 15 minutes **COOK TIME:** 10 minutes

Panzanella is my favorite kind of salad because you get to enjoy lettuce AND delicious chunks of bread. This panzanella is the perfect summertime combination of grilled bread and peaches tossed with fresh basil and arugula.

For the dressing

$1/3$ cup olive oil

2 tablespoons red wine vinegar

$1/2$ teaspoon salt

$1/4$ teaspoon freshly ground black pepper

For the salad

1 loaf French bread, cut into 1-inch cubes

4 tablespoons olive oil, divided

4 peaches, pitted and sliced

1 tablespoon honey

$1/2$ red onion, thinly sliced

$1/2$ cup chopped fresh basil

2 cups fresh arugula

8 ounces fresh mozzarella balls

1. **Preheat the grill.** Preheat the grill to medium-high heat.

2. **Prepare the dressing.** While the grill heats, in a small bowl, whisk the oil, vinegar, salt, and pepper until combined. Set aside.

3. **Prepare the bread.** In a large bowl, toss together the bread cubes and 3 tablespoons of the oil.

4. **Prepare the peaches.** In a medium bowl, toss together the peach slices, the remaining 1 tablespoon of oil, and the honey.

5. **Grill the bread cubes and peaches.** Place the bread cubes in a grill pan and grill for about 5 minutes, turning occasionally, until lightly toasted. While the bread grills, grill the peach slices directly on the grill grates for 2 to 3 minutes per side.

6. **Prepare the salad base.** In a large bowl, combine the toasted bread, grilled peaches, onion, basil, arugula, and mozzarella.

7. **Finish.** Drizzle the dressing over the salad and gently toss to combine.

Smart Shopping: If peaches aren't in season, use frozen peaches. Simply thaw them and grill as you would fresh peaches.

Per Serving: Calories: 575; Saturated Fat: 12g; Total Fat: 41g; Protein: 16g; Total Carbs: 42g; Fiber: 4g; Sodium: 585mg

CRUNCHY ASIAN CHOPPED KALE SALAD

SERVES: 4 | PREP TIME: 25 minutes |

There's always some type of ramen salad at every potluck, and after spotting one at a work gathering one day, I thought, "How can I make this healthier and tastier?" My answer: kale, avocado, fresh mango, and less sugar in the dressing. This salad is infinitely better tasting and always a huge hit at our dinner table.

For the dressing

½ cup rice vinegar

⅓ cup grapeseed or canola oil

⅓ cup honey

2 tablespoons soy sauce

1 tablespoon sesame oil

1 garlic clove, minced

1 teaspoon minced peeled fresh ginger

For the salad

½ head cabbage, finely chopped

3 cups chopped kale

1 cup shelled edamame

1 cup chow mein noodles

1 avocado, peeled, pitted, and diced

1 mango, peeled and diced

½ cup slivered almonds

1. **Prepare the dressing.** In a Mason jar or other lidded airtight container, combine the vinegar, grapeseed or canola oil, honey, soy sauce, sesame oil, garlic, and ginger. Cover and shake well to combine. Set aside.

2. **Prepare the salad base.** In a large bowl, combine the cabbage, kale, edamame, noodles, avocado, mango, and almonds.

3. **Finish.** Pour about ½ the dressing over the salad and stir well to combine. Taste and add more dressing, as needed.

Smart Shopping: Look for shelled edamame in your grocery store's freezer section to reduce prep time!

Per Serving: Calories: 644; Saturated Fat: 4g; Total Fat: 40g; Protein: 12g; Total Carbs: 63g; Fiber: 11g; Sodium: 548mg

MEXICAN STREET CORN PASTA SALAD

SERVES: 4 to 6 | PREP TIME: 15 minutes COOK TIME: 15 minutes

Mexican street corn, also called *elote*, is corn on the cob that is grilled, slathered in mayonnaise and Cotija cheese, and sprinkled with spices and, sometimes, cilantro. It's pure deliciousness. This recipe is elote in pasta salad form—a perfect dish to take to a barbecue.

For the dressing

½ cup mayonnaise

¼ cup plain yogurt

1 tablespoon freshly squeezed lime juice

1 tablespoon chili powder

2 teaspoons ground cumin

½ teaspoon salt

For the pasta salad

8 ounces (about 2 cups) rotini or penne pasta

1 tablespoon canola oil

3 cups (about 14 ounces) frozen corn

1 jalapeño pepper, seeded and diced

3 scallions, chopped

½ cup Cotija cheese or feta cheese

¼ cup chopped fresh cilantro

1. Boil the water. Bring a large pot of water to a boil over high heat.

2. Prepare the dressing. While the water heats, in a small bowl, stir together the mayonnaise, yogurt, lime juice, chili powder, cumin, and salt. Cover and refrigerate until needed.

3. Cook the pasta. Add the pasta to the boiling water and cook according to the package directions. Drain the cooked pasta and rinse it under cold water for 1 minute. Set aside.

4. Cook the corn. While the pasta cooks, heat the oil in a medium skillet over medium-high heat. Add the corn and cook for about 10 minutes, stirring occasionally, until it begins to turn golden and get a little charred in spots.

5. Finish. In a large bowl, combine the cooked pasta, corn, jalapeño, scallions, and dressing. Gently toss to combine and top with the Cotija cheese and cilantro.

Make It Faster: If you're short on time, skip cooking the corn on the stovetop and just thaw it in the microwave before adding to the salad.

Per Serving: Calories: 583; Saturated Fat: 7g; Total Fat: 31g; Protein: 14g; Total Carbs: 65g; Fiber: 6g; Sodium: 729mg

ROASTED RED PEPPER GAZPACHO

SERVES: 4 | PREP TIME: 10 minutes |

Gazpacho is a cold soup made from raw vegetables, which means there's no waiting around for anything to cook. This soup is so full of flavor that it might have you questioning why you should even bother to make hot soup! (Well, maybe not those of us who live in Minnesota.)

2 cucumbers, peeled and ends trimmed, divided

1 (16-ounce) jar roasted red peppers

2 large beefsteak tomatoes, quartered

4 scallions, chopped

4 garlic cloves, minced

¼ cup olive oil

2 tablespoons red wine vinegar

1 teaspoon salt

½ teaspoon freshly ground black pepper

2 tablespoons chopped fresh basil

1. **Prep the cucumber.** Cut about ¼ off one of the cucumbers, dice it, and set aside.

2. **Prepare the soup.** In a blender, combine the remaining cucumbers, peppers, tomatoes, scallions, garlic, oil, vinegar, salt, and pepper. Purée for 60 to 90 seconds, or until smooth.

3. **Finish.** Ladle the gazpacho into 4 bowls and top with the basil and reserved cucumber.

Make It Yourself: If you have extra time, make your own Roasted Red Peppers (page 141).

Per Serving: Calories: 188; Saturated Fat: 2g; Total Fat: 13g; Protein: 3g; Total Carbs: 18g; Fiber: 4g; Sodium: 832mg

CHIPOTLE BLACK BEAN SOUP

SERVES: 4 | PREP TIME: 5 minutes COOK TIME: 15 minutes |

Canned beans make this black bean soup a breeze to whip up. I love using chipotle peppers in adobo sauce (which you can find in the international foods aisle of most grocery stores, or in specialty Mexican grocers) for a blast of flavor and a kick of spice. A dollop of sour cream or plain Greek yogurt on top perfectly balances the smoky spiciness of the chipotles.

1 tablespoon olive oil

1 white onion, chopped

1 (4-ounce) can diced green chiles

2 garlic cloves, minced

2 teaspoons ground cumin

3 (15-ounce) cans black beans, rinsed and drained

4 cups vegetable broth

1 chipotle pepper in adobo sauce

Fresh cilantro, for topping

Sour cream, for topping

1. **Cook the onion.** In a large soup pot over medium-high heat, heat the oil. Add the onion and cook for about 5 minutes, or until translucent.

2. **Add the chiles.** Add the green chiles, garlic, and cumin, and cook for 1 minute more.

3. **Add the black beans.** Stir in the beans, broth, and chipotle. Bring to a simmer and cook the soup for 5 minutes.

4. **Purée the soup.** Using an immersion blender, purée the ingredients until your desired consistency is reached. I like to keep a few chunks in the soup for a little texture.

5. **Finish.** Top each serving with the cilantro and sour cream.

Love Your Leftovers: To save the rest of the can of chipotle peppers, transfer them to a plastic baggie and freeze them. When you need some again, just cut off a chunk!

Per Serving: Calories: 536; Saturated Fat: 3g; Total Fat: 10g; Protein: 34g; Total Carbs: 81g; Fiber: 29g; Sodium: 936mg

SHRIMP TORTILLA SOUP

SERVES: 4 to 6 | PREP TIME: 10 minutes COOK TIME: 15 minutes |

You are likely familiar with chicken tortilla soup, but let me introduce you to your new favorite version: Shrimp Tortilla Soup! I love shrimp as a weeknight protein because it cooks incredibly fast. Instead of having to wait 15 minutes for the chicken to cook, you add the shrimp at the end and boil it for just a few minutes. Of course, tortilla soup is all about the toppings, and they are loaded on in this recipe—all finished with a squeeze of lime.

1 tablespoon olive oil

1 white onion, diced

1 jalapeño pepper, seeded and diced

2 garlic cloves, minced

4 cups vegetable broth

2 cups frozen corn

1 (14.5-ounce) can fire-roasted diced tomatoes

2 tablespoons chili powder

1 tablespoon ground cumin

1 teaspoon salt

1 pound (16 to 20 count) raw peeled and deveined shrimp

¼ cup chopped fresh cilantro

1 avocado, peeled, pitted, and diced

Tortilla strips, for topping

Shredded Cheddar cheese, for topping

1 lime, cut into 6 slices, for topping

1. **Cook the onion and jalapeño.** In a large soup pot over medium-high heat, heat the oil. Add the onion and jalapeño and cook for about 5 minutes, or until they begin to soften.

2. **Add the garlic.** Add the garlic and cook for 1 minute more.

3. **Prepare the broth.** Stir in the broth, corn, tomatoes, chili powder, cumin, and salt. Bring the mixture to a light boil.

4. **Cook the shrimp.** Once boiling, add the shrimp and cook for about 3 minutes, or until they curl and become opaque.

5. **Finish.** Serve the soup topped with the cilantro, avocado, tortilla strips, Cheddar cheese, and a squeeze of lime juice.

Make It Yourself: If you have some homemade Taco Seasoning Mix (page 136) on hand, use 2 tablespoons in place of the chili powder and cumin.

Per Serving: Calories: 414; Saturated Fat: 5g; Total Fat: 14g; Protein: 37g; Total Carbs: 29g; Fiber: 9g; Sodium: 1,804mg

LEMON CHICKPEA AND ORZO SOUP

SERVES: 4 | **PREP TIME:** 7 minutes **COOK TIME:** 20 minutes |

I like to think of this soup as the vegetarian version of chicken noodle soup, but it's so good that you'll love it even if you're an omnivore. This soup is bright from the lemon zest and juice, and hearty thanks to the vegetables and their broth. You can play around with the kind of pasta you use, but I love orzo for its delicate texture that contrasts with the sturdier chickpeas.

1 tablespoon olive oil

1 white onion, diced

2 carrots, peeled and diced

1 celery stalk, diced

2 garlic cloves, minced

1 teaspoon salt

½ teaspoon freshly ground
   black pepper

4 cups vegetable broth

1 (14-ounce) can chickpeas,
   rinsed and drained

½ cup dried orzo

Zest of 1 lemon

Juice of 1 lemon

3 cups fresh baby
   spinach leaves

2 tablespoons fresh dill

1. **Sauté the vegetables.** In a medium skillet over medium-high heat, heat the oil. Add the onion, carrots, celery, garlic, salt, and pepper. Cook for 5 to 7 minutes, or until softened.

2. **Cook the orzo.** Stir in the broth, chickpeas, orzo, lemon zest, and lemon juice. Bring to a simmer and cook until the orzo is done, about 7 minutes.

3. **Add the spinach.** Add the spinach and cook for 1 to 2 minutes, stirring, until wilted.

4. **Finish.** Add the dill and stir to combine.

Per Serving: Calories: 345; Saturated Fat: 1g; Total Fat: 8g; Protein: 18g; Total Carbs: 52g; Fiber: 10g; Sodium: 1,398mg

CREAMY WHITE CHICKEN LASAGNA SOUP

SERVES: 4 to 6 | **PREP TIME:** 10 minutes **COOK TIME:** 20 minutes

Lasagna can be tricky, complicated, and almost impossible to make on a weeknight. So I say— let's just throw all the ingredients into a soup! This creamy chicken lasagna soup has all the flavors of white chicken lasagna but takes only a fraction of the work. To reduce the overall cooking time, I prepare the lasagna noodles separately while the chicken cooks (instead of cooking them in the soup).

8 lasagna noodles, broken into pieces

2 tablespoons olive oil

1 pound boneless skinless chicken breasts, cut into 1-inch pieces

3 tablespoons butter

¼ cup all-purpose flour

2 cups chicken broth

4 cups half-and-half

1 (14.5-ounce) can diced tomatoes

1 tablespoon Italian seasoning

1 teaspoon garlic powder

1 teaspoon salt

½ teaspoon freshly ground black pepper

4 ounces cream cheese, cut into 1-inch cubes

1 cup shredded Parmesan cheese

¼ cup chopped fresh basil

1. **Cook the lasagna.** Bring a large pot of water to a boil over high heat. Add the lasagna noodles and cook according to the package directions. Drain and rinse under cold water. Set aside.

2. **Cook the chicken.** While the pasta cooks, heat the oil in a large soup pot over medium-high heat. Add the chicken and cook for about 5 minutes, or until browned. Remove the chicken from the pot and set aside.

3. **Prepare the soup base.** Return the soup pot to the heat and add the butter to melt. Add the flour and whisk to combine. Slowly whisk in the broth followed by the half-and-half.

4. **Add the tomatoes and seasoning.** Add the tomatoes, Italian seasoning, garlic powder, salt, and pepper. Stir to combine.

5. **Add the cheese.** Bring the mixture to a simmer and add the cream cheese and Parmesan cheese, stirring until they melt.

6. **Finish.** Add the cooked lasagna noodles and the chicken to the pot. Stir to combine and cook for 1 to 2 minutes, or until warmed through. Serve the soup topped with the basil.

Make It Healthier: Use milk in place of half-and-half, and low-fat cream cheese to reduce the fat in this recipe. You can also add 3 cups chopped fresh spinach leaves with the chicken and lasagna noodles to finish with a nutrient boost.

Make It Yourself: This soup would be a great use for leftover Perfect Whole Roasted Chicken (page 144).

Per Serving: Calories: 1,103; Saturated Fat: 34g; Total Fat: 66g; Protein: 57g; Total Carbs: 73g; Fiber: 2g; Sodium: 1,531mg

CHAPTER FOUR
HANDHELDS

Food is just more fun when you don't need a fork to eat it. Burgers, wraps, tacos, and sandwiches are all included in this chapter, but these aren't your typical recipes. You'll find Korean Barbecue Chicken Tacos (page 54), Barbecue Bacon Salmon Burgers (page 53), Eggplant Parmesan Sandwiches (page 61), and Bánh Mì Turkey Burgers (page 58), to name a few. These recipes might be utensil-less, but they're definitely full of flavor!

CAPRESE GARLIC BREAD

SERVES: 4 | PREP TIME: 5 minutes COOK TIME: 3 minutes |

Sometimes the simplest ingredients make the most flavorful meals. The combination of fresh mozzarella, fresh basil, and diced tomatoes here just cannot be beat—and the fact that this dish takes less than 10 minutes to make is nice, too. This recipe uses canned diced tomatoes to reduce prep time.

1 (1-pound) loaf
French bread

2 to 3 tablespoons butter,
at room temperature

1 teaspoon garlic salt

1 (14-ounce) can diced
tomatoes, drained

8 ounces fresh mozzarella
cheese, sliced

¼ cup chopped fresh basil

1. **Preheat the broiler.** Turn the broiler to high.

2. **Prepare the bread.** Cut the bread lengthwise down the center, then cut each half crosswise. Place the bread slices on a baking sheet. Spread the butter on them and season each with garlic salt.

3. **Add the toppings.** Place the tomatoes on the bread and top with the mozzarella.

4. **Broil.** Place the caprese bread under the broiler for 1 to 3 minutes, keeping a very close eye, until the cheese is melted and bubbling.

5. **Finish.** Serve topped with the basil.

Serving Tip: Pair with the Strawberry Avocado Salad (page 33) for a well-rounded, delicious vegetarian meal.

Per Serving: Calories: 568; Saturated Fat: 12g; Total Fat: 19g; Protein: 24g; Total Carbs: 68g; Fiber: 4g; Sodium: 1,027mg

SUMMER VEGETABLE AND GOAT CHEESE WRAPS WITH BASIL DRESSING

SERVES: 4 | **PREP TIME:** 10 minutes | 🍳 ⏰

I make batches of this basil dressing almost weekly in the summer to put on ALL things. It's amazing on BLTs and for dipping grilled vegetables, but my favorite use is in this summer vegetable wrap. The vegetables aren't cooked, making the wraps gloriously crunchy and fresh.

For the basil dressing

½ cup mayonnaise

¼ cup fresh basil

1 tablespoon freshly squeezed lemon juice

2 garlic cloves, peeled

¼ teaspoon salt

For the wraps

4 whole-wheat tortillas

1 zucchini, thinly sliced

1 large tomato, sliced

1 yellow or orange bell pepper, seeded and thinly sliced

1 cup fresh baby spinach leaves

4 ounces goat cheese, crumbled

1. **Prepare the dressing.** In a blender, combine the mayonnaise, basil, lemon juice, garlic, and salt. Purée until smooth.

2. **Finish.** Place the tortillas on a work surface and spread each with ¼ of the basil mayonnaise. Top each with the zucchini, tomato, pepper, and spinach, and sprinkle the cheese over the top. Wrap the tortillas up like a burrito and serve.

Per Serving: Calories: 391; Saturated Fat: 10g; Total Fat: 31g; Protein: 12g; Total Carbs: 18g; Fiber: 3g; Sodium: 451mg

PESTO TURKEY BURGERS

SERVES: 6 | PREP TIME: 5 minutes COOK TIME: 12 minutes

Whenever my basil plant has a growth spurt, I make a big batch of pesto to freeze and cook with for months to come (which I highly recommend doing). These Pesto Turkey Burgers have been a summertime favorite for years, and I always look forward to putting them on the menu. The tangy goat cheese is a great complement to the pesto.

1¼ pounds ground turkey
2 garlic cloves, minced
3 tablespoons jarred pesto, plus more for topping
6 buns
Crumbled goat cheese, for topping
Arugula, for topping

1. **Preheat the grill.** Preheat the grill to medium-high heat.

2. **Form the turkey patties.** In a medium bowl, mix together the turkey, garlic, and pesto until well combined. Form the mixture into 6 patties.

3. **Cook the turkey patties.** Place the patties on the grill and cook for 4 to 5 minutes per side, or until the patties are cooked through and reach an internal temperature of 165°F on an instant-read thermometer.

4. **Finish.** Assemble the burgers: Place the burgers on their bottom buns and top with the cheese, arugula, additional pesto, and the top buns.

Make It Yourself: This recipe uses jarred pesto, but if you have extra time and want to make your own, check out the Pesto recipe (page 137).

Per Serving: Calories: 342; Saturated Fat: 5g; Total Fat: 16g; Protein: 23g; Total Carbs: 24g; Fiber: 1g; Sodium: 463mg

AHI TUNA TACOS WITH MANGO SALSA

SERVES: 4 to 6 | **PREP TIME:** 15 minutes **COOK TIME:** 5 minutes

This recipe just screams FRESH! The flavors are super bold and vibrant, and the ingredients are full of fresh produce. These ahi tuna steaks are quickly marinated in a sesame-soy sauce mixture and seared in a skillet or on the grill. The mango salsa is so good that it could be eaten with a spoon—and if there's any leftover, I highly recommend doing just that.

For the tuna

1 to 1½ pounds ahi
   tuna steaks
¼ cup soy sauce
1 tablespoon olive oil
1 tablespoon sesame oil
2 garlic cloves, minced
1 tablespoon canola oil
8 to 12 corn tortillas

For the mango salsa

2 ripe mangos, peeled
   and diced
½ red onion, finely chopped
¼ cup chopped fresh
   cilantro
1 jalapeño pepper,
   stemmed, seeded,
   and diced
2 tablespoons freshly
   squeezed lime juice
Salt
Freshly ground
   black pepper

1. **Marinate the tuna.** Place the ahi tuna in a shallow bowl or baking dish. In a small bowl, whisk the soy sauce, olive oil, sesame oil, and garlic until combined and pour the marinade over the tuna. Let marinate for 10 minutes.

2. **Prepare the mango salsa.** While the tuna marinates, in a medium bowl, stir together the mango, onion, cilantro, jalapeño, and lime juice, and season with salt and pepper. Set aside.

3. **Cook the tuna.** In a large skillet over medium-high heat, heat the canola oil, or preheat a grill to medium-high heat. Place the tuna in the skillet and sear for 2 minutes per side.

4. **Finish.** Thinly slice the tuna and serve it in the tortillas topped with the salsa.

Per Serving: Calories: 497; Saturated Fat: 2g; Total Fat: 14g; Protein: 45g; Total Carbs: 51g; Fiber: 6g; Sodium: 1,022mg

GRUYÈRE AND ROASTED RED PEPPER TUNA MELTS

SERVES: 4 | PREP TIME: 10 minutes COOK TIME: 10 minutes

I get my love of good tuna melts from my mom. I'm always looking for ways to jazz them up, and here we have the jazziest combo of all—a handful of roasted red peppers and some flavorful Gruyère cheese, both of which add a ton of flavor. This recipe keeps my love of tuna melts going strong!

8 slices bread

2 tablespoons butter, at room temperature

15 ounces canned tuna, drained

¼ cup diced jarred roasted red peppers, drained

2 scallions, chopped

3 tablespoons mayonnaise

1 tablespoon Dijon mustard

1 tablespoon freshly squeezed lemon juice

½ teaspoon salt

¼ teaspoon freshly ground black pepper

4 slices Gruyère cheese

1. **Preheat a griddle and prepare the bread.** Heat a large griddle over medium heat. Place the bread on a work surface and butter the top side.

2. **Prepare the tuna filling.** In a bowl, stir together the tuna, peppers, scallions, mayonnaise, mustard, lemon juice, salt, and pepper.

3. **Assemble the sandwiches.** Turn 4 bread slices over, buttered-side down, and evenly divide the tuna on top of these slices. Place a slice of Gruyère on each sandwich and top with the remaining bread, buttered-side up.

4. **Finish.** Place the sandwiches on the griddle and cook for 4 to 5 minutes per side, until golden brown and the cheese melts.

Make It Yourself: If you have extra time, make your own Roasted Red Peppers (page 141).

Per Serving: Calories: 564; Saturated Fat: 12g; Total Fat: 32g; Protein: 40g; Total Carbs: 28g; Fiber: 2g; Sodium: 893mg

CHICKEN TERIYAKI WRAPS

SERVES: 4 to 6 | PREP TIME: 10 minutes COOK TIME: 15 minutes

When I was in high school, I ate a chicken teriyaki sub from Subway probably every day. After soccer practice, during lunch hour, before a football game, WHENEVER! These days I prefer to make my own chicken teriyaki wraps and love stuffing them full of veggies. I prefer Annie Chun's brand of teriyaki sauce, as it's lower in sugar than other leading brands.

2 tablespoons olive oil
1 pound boneless skinless
  chicken breasts, cut
  into strips
½ cup bottled teriyaki
  sauce, plus more
  as needed
4 to 6 tortillas
1 carrot, shredded
1 red bell pepper, seeded
  and thinly sliced
Mixed spring greens,
  for serving

1. **Cook the chicken strips.** In a large skillet over medium-high heat, heat the oil. Add the chicken strips and cook for 5 to 7 minutes, or until cooked through.

2. **Add the teriyaki sauce.** Stir in the teriyaki sauce.

3. **Finish.** Place the tortillas on a work surface and divide the chicken among them. Top with the carrot, pepper, and greens. Drizzle with more teriyaki sauce, if desired.

Make It Yourself: If you like, make your own Teriyaki Sauce (page 138). This recipe is great for using leftover Perfect Whole Roasted Chicken (page 144).

Per Serving: Calories: 292; Saturated Fat: 1g; Total Fat: 11g; Protein: 29g; Total Carbs: 21g; Fiber: 3g; Sodium: 1,474mg

BARBECUE BACON SALMON BURGERS

SERVES: 4 | **PREP TIME:** 10 minutes **COOK TIME:** 12 minutes

Fresh salmon burgers get jazzed up with smoky barbecue sauce and bacon in this recipe. These salmon burgers are made with a salmon fillet as opposed to canned salmon, which results in a more flavorful, meatier texture. It is well worth the extra five minutes of preparation time!

4 bacon slices

1 (1½-pound) salmon fillet, skin removed if needed

½ cup bread crumbs

1 large egg

1 scallion, diced

1 tablespoon smoky barbecue sauce, plus more for serving

½ teaspoon salt

1 tablespoon olive oil

4 buns

Lettuce leaves, for serving

1. **Cook the bacon.** Place the bacon in a cold skillet and place the skillet over medium heat. Cook the bacon for 8 to 12 minutes, or to your desired crispiness. Transfer the bacon to paper towels to drain.

2. **Prepare the salmon patties.** Finely chop the salmon and place it in a medium bowl. Add the bread crumbs, egg, scallion, barbecue sauce, and salt. Stir to combine and form the mixture into 4 patties.

3. **Cook the salmon patties.** In a large skillet over medium-high heat, heat the oil. Add the patties and cook for 4 to 5 minutes per side, until they are golden brown and cooked through.

4. **Finish.** Place the patties on the bottom buns and top with the bacon, lettuce, more barbecue sauce, and the top buns.

Smart Shopping: Ask your butcher to remove the salmon skin for you, to decrease your preparation time.

Technique Tip: These burgers can also be made outside on a grill. Simply preheat the grill to medium-high heat while you prepare the salmon burgers. Grill them for 4 to 5 minutes per side.

Per Serving: Calories: 584; Saturated Fat: 7g; Total Fat: 30g; Protein: 42g; Total Carbs: 34g; Fiber: 2g; Sodium: 1,263mg

KOREAN BARBECUE CHICKEN TACOS

SERVES: 4 to 6 | PREP TIME: 10 minutes COOK TIME: 12 minutes

Switch up your typical Taco Tuesday with something different—Korean Barbecue Chicken Tacos! The Korean barbecue sauce is so full of flavor AND made with ingredients that are easy to find. The tacos are topped with kimchi, which is not only delicious but, as a fermented food, also has the benefits of probiotics!

2 tablespoons olive oil

1 pound boneless skinless chicken breasts, cut into 1-inch strips

¼ cup soy sauce

Juice of 1 lime

1 tablespoon light brown sugar

1 tablespoon sesame oil

2 garlic cloves, minced

1 teaspoon minced peeled fresh ginger

1 teaspoon Sriracha

8 corn tortillas

1 cup kimchi, for topping

Fresh cilantro, for topping

1. **Cook the chicken.** In a large skillet over medium-high heat, heat the oil. Add the chicken and cook for 10 minutes, or until golden and cooked through.

2. **Prepare the barbecue sauce.** While the chicken cooks, in a small bowl, whisk the soy sauce, lime juice, brown sugar, sesame oil, garlic, ginger, and Sriracha until combined. Set aside.

3. **Combine.** Once the chicken is cooked, add the barbecue sauce to the chicken and cook for 1 to 2 minutes, or until slightly thickened and warmed.

4. **Finish.** Place the tortillas on a work surface and divide the chicken among them. Top with the kimchi and cilantro.

Per Serving: Calories: 392; Saturated Fat: 2g; Total Fat: 15g; Protein: 28g; Total Carbs: 36g; Fiber: 8g; Sodium: 1,776mg

EVERYTHING BAGEL SEASONING CHICKEN SALAD SANDWICHES

SERVES: 4 | PREP TIME: 10 minutes COOK TIME: 15 minutes |

Everything bagel seasoning has quickly become an obsession in our household. We put it on avocado toast, on eggs, and now in our chicken salad. I find mine at Trader Joe's or Costco, but I've seen it at other local grocery stores as well.

1 pound boneless skinless chicken breasts, each piece cut into thirds

3 tablespoons plain whole-milk Greek yogurt

2 tablespoons mayonnaise

1 tablespoon everything bagel seasoning

Bread, croissants, or mixed greens, for serving (optional)

1. **Boil the water.** Bring a large pot of water to a boil over high heat.

2. **Cook the chicken.** Add the chicken to the boiling water and boil for 10 minutes, or until cooked through.

3. **Shred the chicken.** Remove the chicken from the pot and transfer to a work surface. Using 2 forks, shred the chicken and place it in a medium bowl.

4. **Prepare the chicken salad.** Stir in the yogurt, mayonnaise, and everything bagel seasoning, stirring until combined.

5. **Finish.** Serve as a sandwich, in a croissant, or on top of greens, as you like.

Make It Faster: To eliminate the cooking time, making this a super-fast meal, use canned or precooked chicken. This recipe is great for using leftover Perfect Whole Roasted Chicken (page 144).

Per Serving: Calories: 183; Saturated Fat: 1g; Total Fat: 8g; Protein: 25g; Total Carbs: 1g; Fiber: 0g; Sodium: 386mg

CUBAN BURGERS

SERVES: 4 | PREP TIME: 10 minutes COOK TIME: 15 minutes

We all have those menu items we are just suckers for, and, yes, the Cuban sandwich is mine. I just cannot resist the combination of pork, ham, pickles, and mustard. In this recipe, I swapped out the pork for beef, and, I have to say, I think this combination is even better. If you're feeling like a little extra (I know you are!), grill the buns before assembling the burgers.

1 pound ground beef

1 teaspoon garlic powder

1 teaspoon ground cumin

½ teaspoon smoked paprika

½ teaspoon salt

½ teaspoon freshly ground black pepper

4 slices ham

4 slices provolone cheese

4 buns

4 tablespoons mayonnaise

2 tablespoons yellow mustard

4 sandwich pickle slices

1. **Preheat the grill.** Preheat the grill to medium-high heat.

2. **Prepare the beef patties.** In a medium bowl, combine the beef, garlic powder, cumin, paprika, salt, and pepper. Mix to blend and form the meat mixture into 4 patties.

3. **Cook the beef patties.** Place the patties on the grill and cook for 6 to 7 minutes per side. For the last 2 minutes of cooking on the second side, top the burgers with the ham and provolone and close the grill to melt the cheese.

4. **Grill the buns (optional).** Place the buns on the grill for the last 2 minutes of cooking as well.

5. **Finish.** Spread each of the buns with 1 tablespoon of the mayonnaise and 1½ teaspoons of the mustard. Place the patties on the bottom buns and top with the pickles and the top buns.

Smart Shopping: Buy your ham and cheese from the deli counter so you can get the exact amount you need and not have to worry about leftovers!

Per Serving: Calories: 525; Saturated Fat: 11g; Total Fat: 30g; Protein: 39g; Total Carbs: 25g; Fiber: 2g; Sodium: 1,592mg

JALAPEÑO BACON GRILLED CHEESE SANDWICHES

SERVES: 4 | PREP TIME: 5 minutes COOK TIME: 20 minutes | 5

Five ingredients and about 20 minutes are all that stand between you and this smoky, spicy grilled cheese sandwich. The jalapeños make it spicy—and the Pepper Jack kicks up the heat even more. This grilled cheese isn't for the weak!

8 bacon slices

2 tablespoons butter, at room temperature

8 slices bread

1 jalapeño pepper, thinly sliced

8 slices Pepper Jack cheese

1. **Cook the bacon.** Place the bacon in a cold skillet and place the skillet over medium heat. Cook the bacon for 8 to 12 minutes, or to your desired crispiness. Transfer the bacon to paper towels to drain. Reserve the skillet.

2. **Assemble the sandwiches.** Butter one side of each slice of bread. Turn 4 pieces over, buttered-side down, and distribute the jalapeño and cheese evenly over each. Place two pieces of cooked bacon on top of the cheese and top each with a remaining piece of bread, buttered-side up.

3. **Finish.** Remove the bacon grease from the skillet and wipe it clean. Place the skillet over medium heat, add the sandwiches, and cook for 3 to 4 minutes per side, or until golden brown and the cheese melts.

Per Serving: Calories: 531; Saturated Fat: 16g; Total Fat: 33g; Protein: 26g; Total Carbs: 28g; Fiber: 1g; Sodium: 1,599mg

BÁNH MÌ TURKEY BURGERS

SERVES: 4 | PREP TIME: 10 minutes COOK TIME: 15 minutes

I love a good bánh mì sandwich, but making the pork takes a really long time. These Bánh Mì Turkey Burgers have all the flavors of a bánh mì—think quick-pickled veggies and spicy mayonnaise—but only take a fraction of the time!

For the pickled vegetables

1 carrot, shredded

½ cucumber, cut into matchsticks

1 jalapeño pepper, thinly sliced

2 teaspoons salt

1 teaspoon sugar

½ cup white vinegar

½ cup water

For the turkey burgers

1¼ pounds ground turkey

2 scallions, chopped

2 garlic cloves, minced

1½ teaspoons Sriracha

1 teaspoon minced peeled fresh ginger

1 large egg

¼ cup plain bread crumbs

½ teaspoon salt

2 tablespoons canola oil

4 buns

Fresh cilantro, for topping

1. **Pickle the vegetables.** In a medium bowl, combine the carrot, cucumber, jalapeño, salt, sugar, vinegar, and water. Gently stir to combine. Cover and refrigerate until ready to serve.

2. **Prepare the turkey burgers.** In a medium bowl, mix together the turkey, scallion, garlic, Sriracha, ginger, egg, bread crumbs, and salt until combined. Form the meat mixture into four patties.

3. **Cook the turkey burgers.** In a large skillet over medium-high heat, heat the oil. Add the burgers and cook for 5 to 6 minutes per side, or until they're cooked through and reach an internal temperature of 165°F on an instant-read thermometer.

For the spicy mayo

½ **cup mayonnaise**

1 tablespoon Sriracha

4. **Prepare the spicy mayo.** While the burgers cook, in a small bowl, stir together the mayonnaise and Sriracha. Set aside.

5. **Finish.** Top the bottom buns with the burgers, spicy mayo, pickled veggies, cilantro, and the top buns.

Make It Faster: Use jarred pickled vegetables instead of making your own to reduce prep time.

Per Serving: Calories: 583; Saturated Fat: 6g; Total Fat: 32g; Protein: 32g; Total Carbs: 39g; Fiber: 2g; Sodium: 2,096mg

SHRIMP AND ARTICHOKE QUESADILLAS

SERVES: 4 | PREP TIME: 5 minutes COOK TIME: 25 minutes

Because quesadillas are always a hit with my kids, I've become pretty creative with all the fillings. These quesadillas have a creamy shrimp and artichoke filling, made with Greek yogurt and cream cheese and finished with a sprinkle of mozzarella cheese!

4 tablespoons olive oil, divided

8 ounces (16 to 20 count) raw peeled and deveined shrimp

½ cup plain whole-milk Greek yogurt

4 ounces cream cheese, at room temperature

1 (4-ounce) can artichoke hearts, drained and chopped

½ teaspoon garlic powder

½ teaspoon salt

6 flour tortillas

1 cup shredded mozzarella cheese

1. **Cook the shrimp.** In a large skillet over medium-high heat, heat 2 tablespoons of oil. Add the shrimp and cook for about 5 minutes, or until opaque and no longer translucent, turning once about halfway through the cooking time. Remove the shrimp from the skillet and chop them into bite-size pieces. Reserve the skillet.

2. **Prepare the filling.** While the shrimp cook, in a small bowl, stir together the yogurt, cream cheese, artichokes, garlic powder, and salt.

3. **Assemble the quesadillas.** Place the tortillas on a work surface and spread the cream cheese mixture on three of them. Top the cream cheese mixture with the shrimp and mozzarella cheese and then with the remaining tortillas.

4. **Finish.** Wipe out the skillet, place it over medium-high heat, and heat the remaining 2 tablespoons of oil. Working in batches, cook each quesadilla for 4 to 5 minutes per side, or until golden brown.

Technique Tip: Use a large griddle to cook the quesadillas, if you have one. It will hold all the quesadillas and reduce the overall cooking time.

Per Serving: Calories: 462; Saturated Fat: 12g; Total Fat: 31g; Protein: 27g; Total Carbs: 23g; Fiber: 4g; Sodium: 685mg

EGGPLANT PARMESAN SANDWICHES

SERVES: 4 | **PREP TIME:** 15 minutes **COOK TIME:** 15 minutes

Eggplant Parmesan can be tedious to make—but, when made into a sandwich, it's actually pretty easy. (Aren't sandwiches the best?) The breaded eggplant is quickly pan-fried and then deliciously sandwiched between chewy ciabatta buns and topped with marinara and fresh mozzarella.

1 small eggplant, cut into ¼-inch-thick slices

Salt

½ cup all-purpose flour

2 large eggs

1 cup Italian-seasoned bread crumbs

3 tablespoons olive oil

4 ciabatta buns, split

½ cup jarred marinara sauce

4 ounces fresh mozzarella, sliced

¼ cup chopped fresh basil

1. **Prepare the eggplant.** Lay the eggplant on a plate and sprinkle it with salt. Let sit for 5 minutes.

2. **Prepare the batter station.** Place the flour into a shallow bowl. Place the eggs into another shallow bowl and whisk. Place the bread crumbs into a third shallow bowl.

3. **Heat the skillet.** Place a large skillet over medium-high heat and heat the oil.

4. **Cook the eggplant.** Use a paper towel to blot off the moisture from the eggplant and wipe off any excess salt. Coat each slice in flour, eggs, and bread crumbs. Immediately place the coated slices into the heated skillet and cook for about 5 minutes per side, or until they are golden brown.

5. **Preheat the broiler.** While the eggplant cooks, turn the broiler to high.

6. **Assemble the sandwiches.** Place two slices of eggplant on each ciabatta bun bottom. Top each with 2 tablespoons of the marinara, and ¼ of the mozzarella.

7. **Cook the sandwiches.** Place the sandwiches, open-faced, on a baking sheet and under the broiler for 1 minute, or until the cheese is bubbly and golden brown.

8. **Finish.** Sprinkle with the basil and add the ciabatta bun tops.

Make It Yourself: If you want to make your own marinara, check out the recipe for Easy Tomato Pasta Sauce (page 143).

Per Serving: Calories: 614; Saturated Fat: 7g; Total Fat: 23g; Protein: 22g; Total Carbs: 80g; Fiber: 8g; Sodium: 1,385mg

VIETNAMESE BEEF LETTUCE WRAPS WITH PEANUT SAUCE

SERVES: 4 | **PREP TIME:** 20 minutes **COOK TIME:** 10 minutes

Sesame oil is a staple in my pantry because it adds so much flavor. I use it in both the ground beef mixture and the peanut sauce in this recipe. This dish might seem like it has a lot going on, but each component uses very similar ingredients, so just read the recipe first to get your game plan.

For the peanut sauce

⅓ cup peanut butter
1 tablespoon soy sauce
1 tablespoon sesame oil
1 garlic clove, minced
1 teaspoon minced peeled
　fresh ginger
Juice of ½ lime
1 tablespoon honey
2 to 4 tablespoons water

For the wraps

1 pound ground beef
1 cucumber, peeled
　and diced
1 carrot, peeled and
　shredded
1 head romaine or
　Bibb lettuce

1. **Prepare the peanut sauce.** In a food processor, combine the peanut butter, soy sauce, oil, garlic, ginger, lime juice, honey, and 2 tablespoons of water. Blend until smooth. Adjust the consistency of the sauce, adding more water, 1 tablespoon at a time, until your desired consistency is reached. Transfer to a bowl and set aside.

2. **Cook the ground beef.** Heat a large skillet over medium-high heat. Add the ground beef and cook for 5 to 7 minutes, breaking up large chunks with the back of a wooden spoon as it cooks, until it is no longer pink.

For the soy sauce

2 tablespoons soy sauce

1 tablespoon sesame oil

1 garlic clove, minced

1 teaspoon minced peeled
    fresh ginger

1 teaspoon Sriracha

3. **Prepare the soy sauce mixture.** In a small bowl, whisk the soy sauce, sesame oil, garlic, ginger, and Sriracha until well combined.

4. **Add the soy sauce mixture.** Once the beef is cooked, stir in the soy sauce mixture until incorporated.

5. **Finish.** Serve the beef inside the lettuce, topped with the cucumber and carrot, and drizzled with the peanut sauce.

Make It Faster: Buy shredded carrots to reduce prep time.

Per Serving: Calories: 404; Saturated Fat: 6g; Total Fat: 26g; Protein: 29g; Total Carbs: 18g; Fiber: 3g; Sodium: 886mg

CHAPTER FIVE
VEGETARIAN

Cooking meatless meals does not just mean serving veggie burgers and spaghetti topped with marinara sauce. Not only are meatless meals generally faster to make than meals with meat, but they're also delicious! This chapter is full of creative, healthy, and EASY vegetarian meals that will keep your taste buds dancing, such as Thai Peanut Vegetable Rice Bowls (page 78), Southwestern Stuffed Sweet Potatoes (page 68), and Chickpea and Kale Curry (page 73)!

HUMMUS FLATBREADS

SERVES: 4 | PREP TIME: 15 minutes |

My family's love for hummus knows no limits. We buy a big tub from Costco and go to town on it at an alarming rate. I suppose there are worse things. Because we eat so much of it, I love getting creative with how we eat it, so these flatbreads are a regular on our lunch rotation. They're crunchy, salty, creamy, and so fresh. Drooling now.

¼ cup plain yogurt

1 tablespoon olive oil

1 tablespoon freshly squeezed lemon juice

1 teaspoon dried dill or 1 tablespoon chopped fresh dill

¼ teaspoon salt

4 to 6 pita breads

1 cup hummus

1 small cucumber, sliced

1 cup cherry tomatoes, quartered

½ cup feta cheese

¼ cup Kalamata olives, chopped

1. **Prep the yogurt.** In a small bowl, whisk the yogurt, oil, lemon juice, dill, and salt until combined. Set aside.

2. **Assemble the pitas.** Lay the pitas on a work surface and divide the hummus among them. Top with the cucumber, tomatoes, feta cheese, and olives.

3. **Finish.** Drizzle with the yogurt mixture.

Ingredient Tip: If your pitas are a little hard, microwave them on high power, covered with a damp paper towel, for 30 to 45 seconds to soften them.

Per Serving: Calories: 389; Saturated Fat: 5g; Total Fat: 16g; Protein: 15g; Total Carbs: 49g; Fiber: 6g; Sodium: 1,003mg

SOUTHWESTERN STUFFED SWEET POTATOES

SERVES: 4 | **PREP TIME:** 5 minutes **COOK TIME:** 10 minutes

Sweet potatoes can take a long time to bake, but they're too delicious to pass up. So, for all the sweet potato lovers out there, here's how you can cut your cooking time in half using a microwave. These "baked" sweet potatoes are stuffed with southwestern-spiced beans and corn, and then topped with all the fixins. My favorite part is the crushed tortilla chips, which add the perfect crunch. Yum.

4 sweet potatoes, cleaned

1 (16-ounce) can black beans, rinsed and drained

1 (16-ounce) can corn, rinsed and drained

1 teaspoon chili powder

1 teaspoon ground cumin

Salt

1 avocado, peeled, pitted, and sliced

Salsa, for topping

Sour cream, for topping

Shredded Cheddar cheese, for topping

Crushed tortilla chips, for topping

1. **Cook the sweet potatoes.** Pierce the sweet potatoes about 10 times with a fork. Place them on a plate and microwave them on high power for 8 minutes. Check to see if they are done; if not, microwave for 2 to 3 minutes more. A fork should easily pierce into a sweet potato once it is done.

2. **Prepare the stuffing.** In a bowl, stir together the beans, corn, chili powder, and cumin. Taste and season with salt.

3. **Assemble.** Cut a slit down the center of each cooked sweet potato and squeeze each one open. Fill the potatoes with the black bean stuffing.

4. **Finish.** Top with the avocado, salsa, sour cream, cheese, and crushed tortilla chips.

Make It Healthier: Use plain Greek yogurt instead of sour cream to make this dish even healthier.

Per Serving: Calories: 571; Saturated Fat: 8g; Total Fat: 20g; Protein: 22g; Total Carbs: 84g; Fiber: 21g; Sodium: 632mg

TOMATO AND GOAT CHEESE TART

SERVES: 4 | PREP TIME: 5 minutes COOK TIME: 10 minutes

Make this easy, flavorful tart in the middle of summer, when fresh tomatoes are at their peak! I love using heirloom tomatoes that I find at the farmers' market. Heirloom tomatoes lend a variety of colors and flavors to this tart, making me seem much fancier than I really am. Goat cheese is a fun change from the typical mozzarella that is usually paired with tomatoes and basil, and lends a tangy flavor and creamy texture.

Nonstick cooking spray
1 (8-ounce) can crescent rolls
1 tablespoon butter, melted
1 garlic clove, minced
¼ teaspoon salt
1 large heirloom tomato or 2 Roma tomatoes, thinly sliced
4 ounces crumbled goat cheese
¼ cup chopped fresh basil

1. **Preheat the oven and prepare the baking sheet.** Preheat the oven to 425°F. Coat a baking sheet with cooking spray.

2. **Form the pastry.** On the prepared baking sheet, roll out the crescent dough into one large rectangular tart. Pinch together the seams that go diagonally across each rectangle.

3. **Brush the pastry with butter.** In a small bowl, whisk the melted butter, garlic, and salt until combined. Using a pastry brush, brush the tart with the garlic butter.

4. **Add the tomatoes and cheese.** Lay the tomatoes on top of the garlic butter, leaving a slight edge for the crust. Sprinkle on the cheese.

5. **Bake.** Bake for 8 to 9 minutes, or until the edges are golden brown.

6. **Finish.** Top with the basil.

Serving Tip: Serve this tart with a large side salad, such as the Tuscan Bean and Arugula Salad (page 32), for a well-rounded and satisfying meal.

Per Serving: Calories: 340; Saturated Fat: 10g; Total Fat: 17g; Protein: 15g; Total Carbs: 32g; Fiber: 2g; Sodium: 572mg

CREAMY LEMON TORTELLINI WITH PEAS

SERVES: 4 to 6 | **PREP TIME:** 5 minutes **COOK TIME:** 15 minutes

Tortellini is always a crowd-pleaser, and I love how quickly it cooks. In this dish, I pair cheese-filled tortellini with a light, bright creamy lemon sauce and peas for a quick vegetarian weeknight meal that's comforting and nourishing!

1 (20-ounce) package refrigerated cheese tortellini

1 tablespoon olive oil

1 shallot, finely chopped

2 cups whole milk

1 cup vegetable broth

1 teaspoon lemon zest

½ teaspoon salt

½ teaspoon freshly ground black pepper

1 cup shredded mozzarella cheese

1 cup frozen peas

1. **Cook the tortellini.** Bring a large pot of water to a boil over high heat. Add the tortellini and cook according to the package directions. Drain.

2. **Prepare the pasta sauce.** While the tortellini cooks, heat the oil in a medium saucepan over medium heat. Add the shallot and cook for about 5 minutes, or until softened. Slowly whisk in the milk and broth. Whisk in the lemon zest, salt, and pepper, and bring the mixture to a simmer.

3. **Add the cheese.** Add the cheese to the mixture and stir until melted. Cook the sauce until it is slightly thickened, 3 to 4 minutes more.

4. **Finish.** Add the tortellini and peas to the sauce. Cook for 1 to 2 minutes to heat the peas and incorporate the sauce into the pasta.

Per Serving: Calories: 663; Saturated Fat: 10g; Total Fat: 25g; Protein: 35g; Total Carbs: 75g; Fiber: 8g; Sodium: 1,347mg

PENNE WITH PUTTANESCA SAUCE

SERVES: 4 to 6 | PREP TIME: 5 minutes COOK TIME: 15 minutes

Puttanesca sauce is an Italian pasta sauce typically made with olives, capers, red pepper flakes, and anchovies. I took out the anchovies to make it vegetarian, and it turned out just as delicious. I can only make this sauce sparingly in our house, as my husband despises olives and capers, but believe me—every time he works the night shift at the hospital, it's just me and this sauce.

8 to 10 ounces penne pasta

2 tablespoons extra-virgin olive oil

4 garlic cloves, minced

1 teaspoon red pepper flakes

1 (28-ounce) can crushed tomatoes

1 cup cherry tomatoes

¼ cup chopped Kalamata olives

2 tablespoons chopped fresh basil

1 tablespoon tomato paste

1 tablespoon capers, drained

1 tablespoon butter

1 teaspoon sugar

Salt

Freshly ground black pepper

Fresh parsley, for topping

1. **Cook the pasta.** Bring a large pot of water to a boil over high heat. Add the penne pasta and cook according to the package directions. Drain.

2. **Cook the sauce.** While the pasta cooks, heat the oil in a large saucepan over medium heat. Add the garlic and red pepper flakes and cook for 1 minute. Add the crushed tomatoes, cherry tomatoes, olives, basil, tomato paste, capers, butter, and sugar. Season with salt and pepper and bring the mixture to a simmer. Cook for 10 minutes, or until the cherry tomatoes burst.

3. **Finish.** Serve the cooked penne with the sauce and top with the parsley.

Make It Healthier: Swap the pasta for zucchini noodles to enjoy this delicious sauce in an even healthier way.

Per Serving: Calories: 407; Saturated Fat: 3g; Total Fat: 12g; Protein: 13g; Total Carbs: 62g; Fiber: 10g; Sodium: 585mg

BROWN-BUTTERED NOODLES WITH KALE AND TOASTED WALNUTS

SERVES: 4 to 6 | PREP TIME: 5 minutes COOK TIME: 15 minutes |

If you've never browned butter, I'm just going to stop you right here and demand you head to your kitchen immediately. Brown butter is a game changer, whether in cookies, brownies, breads, pastas—basically anything that has butter in it. These brown-buttered noodles are my go-to dinner for when I'm cooking just for myself and my boys. I get to enjoy delicious buttery noodles, and I'm getting my kids to eat kale. High five.

1 pound spaghetti noodles

8 tablespoons (1 stick) unsalted butter

1 cup chopped walnuts

½ teaspoon salt

2 cups finely chopped kale, leaves only

½ cup shredded Parmesan cheese

1. **Cook the pasta.** Bring a large pot of water to a boil over high heat. Add the spaghetti and cook according to the package directions. Drain. Reserve the pot.

2. **Brown the butter.** While the pasta cooks, melt the butter in a small saucepan over medium heat (I like to use a light-colored pan so I can see the butter changing color). Cook until it begins to foam and form brown bits, usually around 8 to 10 minutes. Keep an eye on it so it doesn't burn.

3. **Toast the walnuts.** In another small saucepan over medium heat, toast the walnuts for 3 to 5 minutes, shaking the pan a couple of times throughout, until browned and fragrant.

4. **Combine the ingredients.** Return the spaghetti to the pot it was cooked in and place it over medium heat. Add the brown butter, salt, kale, and walnuts. Stir to combine and cook for 2 to 3 minutes, or until the kale is softened.

5. **Finish.** Serve topped with the Parmesan cheese.

Smart Shopping: The better the quality of your butter, the faster it will brown. Higher quality butter has less water and, therefore, less liquid that needs to evaporate before browning. This is an instance when spending an extra couple of dollars will actually cut down on time in the kitchen.

Per Serving: Calories: 876; Saturated Fat: 19g; Total Fat: 46g; Protein: 24g; Total Carbs: 92g; Fiber: 6g; Sodium: 606mg

CHICKPEA AND KALE CURRY

SERVES: 4 to 6 | **PREP TIME:** 5 minutes **COOK TIME:** 15 minutes

People seem surprised when I tell them curry is one of our toddler's favorite meals. My curry is pretty mild and family-friendly. It also comes together shockingly fast, partly because I always keep curry powder in my pantry. Curry powder is a combination of spices, including turmeric, cumin, chili powder, coriander, mustard, ginger, and cinnamon. With curry powder on hand, I can make this chickpea and kale curry whenever the curry craving strikes!

1½ cups rice

3 cups water

1 tablespoon olive oil

1 white onion, diced

1 red bell pepper, seeded and diced

3 cups chopped kale, leaves only

1 (14-ounce) can chickpeas, rinsed and drained

1 tablespoon curry powder

½ teaspoon ground ginger

½ teaspoon salt

1 (14-ounce) can coconut milk

Fresh cilantro, for serving

1. **Cook the rice.** In a medium saucepan, bring the rice and water to a boil over high heat. Reduce the heat to low, cover the pan, and simmer the rice for 15 to 18 minutes, or until the water is absorbed and the rice is tender.

2. **Sauté the onion and bell pepper.** While the rice cooks, heat the oil in a large skillet over medium-high heat. Add the onion and pepper and cook for 5 to 7 minutes, or until softened.

3. **Add the kale and chickpeas.** Stir in the kale, chickpeas, curry powder, ginger, salt, and coconut milk. Cook for 3 to 5 minutes, or until the kale is softened.

4. **Finish.** Ladle the curry over the cooked rice and sprinkle with the cilantro.

Per Serving: Calories: 724; Saturated Fat: 22g; Total Fat: 31g; Protein: 18g; Total Carbs: 99g; Fiber: 13g; Sodium: 340mg

TOMATO BASIL VEGETABLES AND COUSCOUS

SERVES: 4 to 6 | **PREP TIME:** 10 minutes **COOK TIME:** 15 minutes

One of the first foods I cooked in college was couscous, a dish that made me feel fancy. I'm not sure why, as it's insanely easy, but it was something that I had never made (or even eaten) before. Cooking couscous is very different from rice—it allows you to multitask without having to worry about checking it every few minutes, which means you can focus on cooking the vegetables. This dish is best made in summer, when these vegetables are at their peak.

3 cups vegetable broth

2 cups couscous

2 tablespoons olive oil

1 shallot, diced

½ teaspoon salt

2 zucchini, thinly sliced

1 summer squash, thinly sliced

1 pint cherry tomatoes, halved

1 cup corn kernels, fresh or frozen

3 garlic cloves, minced

¼ cup chopped fresh basil

1. **Cook the couscous.** In a medium saucepan over high heat, bring the vegetable broth to a boil. Add the couscous, turn off the heat, and cover the pan with a lid. Let sit for 5 to 7 minutes undisturbed. Once ready to serve, fluff the couscous with a fork.

2. **Cook the veggies.** Once the couscous is sitting, in a large skillet over medium-high heat, heat the oil. Add the shallot and salt and cook for about 3 minutes, or until it begins to soften. Add the zucchini, squash, tomatoes, and corn. Cook for about 5 minutes, or until the veggies are softened. Stir in the garlic and basil and cook for 1 minute more.

3. **Finish.** Serve the veggies over the cooked couscous.

Per Serving: Calories: 492; Saturated Fat: 2g; Total Fat: 10g; Protein: 19g; Total Carbs: 85g; Fiber: 7g; Sodium: 897mg

VIETNAMESE NOODLE BOWLS

SERVES: 4 | **PREP TIME:** 15 minutes **COOK TIME:** 10 minutes

Vietnamese noodle bowls are like a vegetarian spring roll in bowl form. Trust me—you'll be licking your bowl clean when the noodles are all gone. Rice noodles are so great for a weeknight meal because they cook super quickly—and because you soak them in hot water, you don't have to worry about them while you prepare the rest of the ingredients.

For the bowls

1 (8-ounce) package
  vermicelli rice noodles
1 cucumber, cut into
  matchsticks
1 carrot, shredded
2 cups finely chopped
  romaine lettuce
Chopped fresh cilantro,
  for topping
Chopped fresh mint,
  for topping
½ cup chopped peanuts,
  for topping

For the dressing

¼ cup rice vinegar
2 tablespoons soy sauce
2 tablespoons canola oil
1 tablespoon honey
2 teaspoons grated peeled
  fresh ginger
2 garlic cloves, minced
Juice of 1 lime

1. **Cook the noodles.** Bring a large pot of water to a boil over high heat. Add the rice noodles, remove the pot from the heat, and let sit to soften, about 10 minutes. Drain and rinse with cold water.

2. **Prepare the dressing.** While the noodles soak, in a small bowl, whisk the vinegar, soy sauce, oil, honey, ginger, garlic, and lime juice until combined. Set aside.

3. **Combine the ingredients.** In a large bowl, stir together the cooked noodles, cucumber, carrot, romaine, and dressing.

4. **Finish.** Serve in individual bowls topped with the cilantro, mint, and peanuts.

Smart Shopping: You can also buy a bag of shredded carrots and chopped romaine instead of shredding and chopping them yourself.

Per Serving: Calories: 425; Saturated Fat: 2g; Total Fat: 16g; Protein: 10g; Total Carbs: 60g; Fiber: 5g; Sodium: 478mg

CHIPOTLE BLACK BEAN ENCHILADAS

SERVES: 4 to 6 | PREP TIME: 10 minutes COOK TIME: 15 minutes |

Enchiladas in less than 30 minutes AND with only 5 ingredients? Yes, this is real life. Although these enchiladas are low in ingredients, they are HIGH in flavor—thanks to a spicy, smoky chipotle-infused black bean mixture. The bean filling is also super easy to make thanks to my trusty food processor, one of my most-used kitchen appliances.

Nonstick cooking spray
2 (16-ounce) cans black beans, rinsed and drained
2 (10-ounce) cans enchilada sauce, divided
2 chipotle peppers in adobo sauce, finely diced
10 corn or flour tortillas
1½ cups shredded Cheddar cheese

1. **Preheat the oven and prepare the pan.** Preheat the oven to 400°F. Spray a 9-by-13-inch baking dish with cooking spray and set aside.

2. **Prepare the bean filling.** In a large food processor, combine the beans, 1 can of the enchilada sauce, and the chipotles. Pulse until about half the beans are puréed, creating a chunky bean paste.

3. **Prepare the pan.** Spread half of the remaining can of enchilada sauce on the bottom of the prepared baking dish.

4. **Assemble the enchiladas.** Place the tortillas on a work surface and evenly distribute the bean filling among them, spreading it out. Roll each into an enchilada and place in the baking dish, seam-side down. Top with the remaining enchilada sauce and the cheese.

5. **Finish.** Bake for 15 minutes, or until the cheese melts and starts to brown. Serve warm.

Per Serving: Calories: 675; Saturated Fat: 10g; Total Fat: 20g; Protein: 36g; Total Carbs: 90g; Fiber: 26g; Sodium: 816mg

HONEY-GINGER VEGETABLE STIR-FRY

SERVES: 4 | **PREP TIME:** 15 minutes **COOK TIME:** 15 minutes

This is one of those meals that will quickly become a regular in your weekly rotation. My husband is typically skeptical of vegetable-based meals, but he couldn't get enough of this one! This stir-fry is very adaptable to different vegetables and grains, so don't be afraid to mix things up. The important thing is the irresistible honey-ginger sauce—don't mess with that part!

For the stir-fry

1½ cups rice

3 cups water, plus 2 tablespoons, divided

3 tablespoons olive oil

1 red onion, sliced

1 yellow bell pepper, seeded and sliced

2 carrots, shredded

1 head broccoli, cut into florets (about 3 cups)

For the honey-ginger sauce

⅓ cup soy sauce

3 tablespoons water

2 tablespoons honey

2 tablespoons rice wine vinegar

2 tablespoons olive oil

2 garlic cloves, minced

1 tablespoon minced peeled fresh ginger

1. **Cook the rice.** In a medium saucepan, bring the rice and 3 cups of the water to a boil over high heat. Reduce the heat to low, cover the pan, and simmer the rice for 15 to 18 minutes, or until the water is absorbed and the rice is tender.

2. **Sauté the vegetables.** In a large wok or skillet over medium-high heat, heat the oil. Add the onion, bell pepper, and carrots. Cook for 5 to 7 minutes, stirring, until softened.

3. **Add the broccoli.** Add the broccoli and the remaining 2 tablespoons of water. Cover the wok with a lid, letting the broccoli cook and steam until tender, about 5 minutes.

4. **Prepare the sauce.** While the vegetables cook, in a medium bowl, whisk the soy sauce, water, honey, vinegar, oil, garlic, and ginger until combined. Set aside.

5. **Add the sauce.** Once the broccoli is cooked, drizzle the vegetables with the honey-ginger sauce, stirring to combine. Cook for 2 to 3 minutes, or until the sauce is slightly thickened.

6. **Finish.** Serve over the cooked rice.

Make It Healthier: Serve with brown rice or quinoa for a healthier, protein-rich grain.

Per Serving: Calories: 511; Saturated Fat: 3g; Total Fat: 18g; Protein: 9g; Total Carbs: 79g; Fiber: 5g; Sodium: 1,247mg

THAI PEANUT VEGETABLE RICE BOWLS

SERVES: 4 | PREP TIME: 15 minutes COOK TIME: 15 minutes

Thai peanut sauce is one of my secret weapons when it comes to getting my kids to eat different foods. They love peanut butter, so, naturally, they love Thai peanut sauce. I'm basically getting them to eat vegetables with "peanut butter sauce" on them. That's a mom win in my book. This recipe is a tasty combination of simple sautéed vegetables and protein-rich healthy fats.

For the rice bowls

2 cups rice

4 cups water

3 tablespoons olive oil

2 cups shredded carrots

2 cups shredded
red cabbage

1 cup sugar snap peas

1 red bell pepper, seeded
and sliced

2 cups chopped kale,
leaves only

¼ cup chopped peanuts

2 scallions, chopped

Fresh cilantro, for topping

For the peanut sauce

1 (14-ounce) can
coconut milk

½ cup peanut butter

2 tablespoons soy sauce

1 tablespoon honey

Juice of 1 lime

1. **Cook the rice.** In a medium saucepan, bring the rice and water to a boil over high heat. Reduce the heat to low, cover the pan, and simmer the rice for 15 to 18 minutes, or until the water is absorbed and the rice is tender.

2. **Cook the vegetables.** While the rice cooks, heat the oil in a large skillet over medium-high heat. Add the carrots, cabbage, peas, and bell peppers. Cook for about 10 minutes, or until softened. During the last 2 minutes of cooking time, add the kale.

3. **Prepare the peanut sauce.** While the veggies cook, combine the coconut milk, peanut butter, soy sauce, honey, and lime juice in a small food processor. Purée until smooth.

4. **Add the peanut sauce.** Once the veggies are cooked, add the peanut sauce to the skillet, stirring well to combine.

5. **Finish.** Serve the vegetables over the cooked rice in 4 bowls. Top each with the peanuts, scallions, and cilantro.

Per Serving: Calories: 984; Saturated Fat: 27g; Total Fat: 56g; Protein: 23g; Total Carbs: 107g; Fiber: 10g; Sodium: 682mg

VEGETABLE FAJITA QUINOA BOWLS

SERVES: 4 to 6 | **PREP TIME:** 10 minutes **COOK TIME:** 20 minutes

Meatless Monday has never tasted better than these fajita bowls, which are full of onions and peppers tossed in fajita spices and served with beans and sliced avocado. Quinoa is also one of my favorite bases for grain bowls because it soaks up any flavors it's paired with. It doesn't hurt that quinoa is full of protein and fiber, either.

2 cups dry quinoa,
  rinsed well
4 cups water
2 tablespoons olive oil
1 red onion, sliced
1 red bell pepper, seeded
  and sliced
1 green bell pepper, seeded
  and sliced
1 yellow bell pepper,
  seeded and sliced
1 (16-ounce) can black
  beans, rinsed and drained
2 garlic cloves, minced
1 tablespoon chili powder
2 teaspoons ground cumin
1 teaspoon salt
1 avocado, peeled, pitted,
  and sliced
1 lime, cut into 4 to 6
  wedges, for serving
Plain Greek yogurt,
  for serving

1. **Cook the quinoa.** In a medium pot, combine the quinoa and water. Bring to a boil, reduce the heat to maintain a simmer, cover the pot, and simmer for 15 to 18 minutes, or until the quinoa is cooked and the water is absorbed.

2. **Sauté the vegetables.** In a large skillet over medium-high heat, heat the oil. Add the onion and peppers and cook for 7 to 8 minutes, or until softened.

3. **Add the beans.** Stir in the beans, garlic, chili powder, cumin, and salt. Cook for 1 to 2 minutes more.

4. **Finish.** Assemble the bowls. Divide the quinoa and vegetables evenly among bowls. Top with the avocado, a squeeze of lime juice, and a dollop of yogurt.

Per Serving: Calories: 661; Saturated Fat: 3g; Total Fat: 20g; Protein: 25g; Total Carbs: 100g; Fiber: 22g; Sodium: 616mg

CHAPTER SIX
SEAFOOD

When it comes to quick-cooking proteins, seafood is one of the fastest. In fact, shrimp can cook in just five minutes! For easy and delicious dinners, look no further. Seafood is also naturally lower in fat and calories than other proteins and is a great healthy option for dinner. You'll be delighted by the flavor you'll find in recipes such as Smoked Salmon Flatbreads (page 84), Chili-Lime Baked Salmon (page 87), Shrimp Tabbouleh (page 89), and Blackened Cod with Corn Salsa (page 88).

TUNA SALAD-STUFFED AVOCADOS

SERVES: 4 | PREP TIME: 10 minutes |

Tuna salad isn't just for elementary school sandwiches anymore! In this recipe, a simple but flavorful tuna salad is stuffed inside an avocado—which is how adults like to handle their problems. Avocados are a great source of healthy fats, potassium, and fiber, and they keep this dish lower in carbs. Prep this for a delicious lunch or a light dinner!

10 ounces canned
   tuna, drained
1 celery stalk, chopped
1 scallion, chopped
1 tablespoon mayonnaise
1 tablespoon plain
   whole-milk Greek yogurt
2 teaspoons Dijon mustard
Salt
Freshly ground
   black pepper
2 avocados, halved
   and pitted
Hot sauce, for serving
   (optional)

1. **Prepare the tuna salad.** In a bowl, stir together the tuna, celery, scallion, mayonnaise, yogurt, and mustard. Season with salt and pepper.

2. **Assemble.** Spoon the tuna salad into the avocados.

3. **Finish.** Drizzle with the hot sauce (if using).

Per Serving: Calories: 302; Saturated Fat: 3g; Total Fat: 22g; Protein: 21g; Total Carbs: 8g; Fiber: 6g; Sodium: 136mg

SMOKED SALMON FLATBREADS

SERVES: 4 | PREP TIME: 10 minutes |

I love visiting my mother-in-law, because she puts smoked salmon on her cheese boards—and I can never get enough of it. These easy, no-bake flatbreads combine the stellar flavors of smoked salmon, cream cheese, and dill atop my favorite base for flatbreads, naan—ready to go and perfectly chewy.

4 ounces cream cheese, at room temperature

1 tablespoon freshly squeezed lemon juice

1 tablespoon sour cream

2 tablespoons chopped fresh dill, plus more for topping

Salt

2 naan

8 ounces thinly sliced smoked salmon

¼ red onion, thinly sliced

2 tablespoons capers, drained

1. **Prepare the cream cheese spread.** In a small bowl, stir together the cream cheese, lemon juice, and sour cream. Stir in 2 tablespoons of the dill. Season with salt.

2. **Assemble the flatbreads.** Place the naan on a work surface and spread the cream cheese mixture onto each.

3. **Distribute the toppings.** Top the cream cheese with slices of salmon and onion. Sprinkle with the capers and top with more fresh dill.

4. **Finish.** Cut into slices and enjoy.

Make It Healthier: Use reduced-fat cream cheese and plain Greek yogurt instead of sour cream to lighten these flatbreads.

Per Serving: Calories: 275; Saturated Fat: 8g; Total Fat: 15g; Protein: 16g; Total Carbs: 19g; Fiber: 1g; Sodium: 1,656mg

TOMATO-BASIL SHRIMP

SERVES: 4 | PREP TIME: 5 minutes COOK TIME: 5 minutes |

Shrimp is awesome for weeknight dinners because it cooks so fast. This simple dish only takes 10 minutes to come together, but it's packed with delicious flavor. This recipe uses canned diced tomatoes with garlic and onion, which lend a ton of flavor with no extra prep time. I also love this dish because it's totally customizable—serve it with whatever you enjoy or have around.

1 tablespoon olive oil

1 pound (16 to 20 count) raw peeled and deveined shrimp

1 (14-ounce) can diced tomatoes with onions and garlic

¼ to ½ teaspoon red pepper flakes, to taste

2 tablespoons chopped fresh basil, for topping

Shredded Parmesan cheese, for topping

1. **Cook the shrimp.** In a large skillet over medium-high heat, heat the oil. Add the shrimp and cook for 3 to 4 minutes, or until pink, turning once about halfway through the cooking time.

2. **Add the tomatoes.** Stir in the tomatoes and red pepper flakes. Cook for 2 minutes to warm through.

3. **Finish.** Serve topped with the basil and Parmesan cheese.

Serving Tip: I love serving this shrimp over couscous or quinoa, but it would also be great with Pan-Sautéed Vegetables (page 140), zucchini noodles (which you can find at some grocery stores), any pasta, or a toasted baguette.

Per Serving: Calories: 186; Saturated Fat: 2g; Total Fat: 6g; Protein: 27g; Total Carbs: 7g; Fiber: 1g; Sodium: 529mg

PAN-SEARED TILAPIA WITH GARLIC BUTTER SAUCE

SERVES: 4 | PREP TIME: 10 minutes COOK TIME: 10 minutes

You can't go wrong with garlic and butter—right?! I love cooking tilapia on weeknights because the fillets are quite thin, meaning they cook really fast. In this recipe the flaky fish is drizzled with a garlic and butter sauce that is indulgent but not heavy. My husband declared this his favorite seafood dish that I've ever made. And I've made a lot.

1 tablespoon olive oil

3 tablespoons butter, divided

$\frac{1}{3}$ cup all-purpose flour

4 tilapia fillets

3 garlic cloves, minced

$\frac{1}{4}$ teaspoon salt

$\frac{1}{3}$ cup dry white wine or cooking wine

2 tablespoons chopped fresh parsley

1. **Preheat a skillet.** In a large skillet over medium-high heat, heat the oil and 1 tablespoon of the butter until it melts.

2. **Prepare the tilapia.** Place the flour in a shallow bowl and dip each tilapia fillet in the flour to dust it lightly. Shake off any excess.

3. **Cook the tilapia.** Add the tilapia to the skillet and cook for 2 to 3 minutes per side, or until the fillets are cooked through. Remove the tilapia from the pan.

4. **Prepare the garlic butter sauce.** Add the remaining 2 tablespoons of butter to the skillet. Once melted, add the garlic and salt. Cook for 1 minute. Add the white wine and cook for 2 to 3 minutes, or until slightly reduced. Remove the skillet from the heat and add the parsley.

5. **Finish.** Serve the tilapia drizzled with the sauce.

Make It Faster: Use jarred minced garlic to reduce prep time.

Serving Tip: I recommend serving this tilapia with microwave-baked potatoes and some steamed vegetables or Pan-Sautéed Vegetables (page 140) for a well-rounded meal.

Per Serving: Calories: 258; Saturated Fat: 6g; Total Fat: 13g; Protein: 22g; Total Carbs: 9g; Fiber: 0g; Sodium: 251mg

CHILI-LIME BAKED SALMON

SERVES: 4 | **PREP TIME:** 5 minutes **COOK TIME:** 15 minutes

My favorite way to serve this chili-lime baked salmon is on top of a premade southwestern chopped salad mix. The mixes usually come with some sort of southwestern ranch dressing and tortilla strips for topping, and I'll throw in some black beans and corn to bulk it up. If you're not in the mood for a salad, make some Pan-Sautéed Vegetables (page 140) while the salmon cooks for a well-rounded, healthy meal.

1 tablespoon olive oil

1 tablespoon freshly squeezed lime juice

1 tablespoon chili powder

1 teaspoon ground cumin

1 teaspoon brown sugar

½ teaspoon garlic powder

¼ teaspoon salt

4 (4- to 6-ounce) salmon fillets

1. **Preheat the oven and prepare the baking sheet.** Preheat oven to 425°F. Line a baking sheet with parchment paper and set aside.

2. **Prepare the chili-lime seasoning.** In a small bowl, stir together the oil, lime juice, chili powder, cumin, brown sugar, garlic powder, and salt until combined.

3. **Prepare the salmon.** Place the salmon on the prepared baking sheet and cover it with the chili-lime mixture.

4. **Bake the salmon.** Bake the salmon for 12 to 16 minutes, depending on the size of the fillets, until it flakes easily with a fork.

5. **Finish.** Serve with any optional side dish you made while the salmon cooks (see introduction).

Per Serving: Calories: 342; Saturated Fat: 4g; Total Fat: 22g; Protein: 33g; Total Carbs: 3g; Fiber: 1g; Sodium: 264mg

BLACKENED COD WITH CORN SALSA

SERVES: 4 | PREP TIME: 10 minutes COOK TIME: 10 minutes

Cod is a great fish for anyone who's on the fence with seafood. Cod is mild in flavor, easy to cook, and takes on whatever flavors you add to it. This recipe uses an easy pantry-staple seasoning blend that is smoky and a little spicy for that perfect blackening flavor. The zippy corn salsa is a great complement to the blackened cod.

For the cod

1 tablespoon chili powder

1 teaspoon smoked paprika

1 teaspoon garlic powder

1 teaspoon dried oregano

½ teaspoon salt

¼ teaspoon cayenne pepper

1 pound cod fillets

2 tablespoons canola oil

For the salsa

2 cups frozen corn, thawed

1 jalapeño pepper, stemmed, seeded, and diced

¼ red onion, diced

¼ cup chopped fresh cilantro

Juice of 1 lime

½ teaspoon ground cumin

¼ teaspoon salt

1. **Prepare the cod.** In a small bowl, whisk the chili powder, paprika, garlic powder, oregano, salt, and cayenne until combined. Sprinkle the cod with the blackening seasoning.

2. **Preheat a skillet.** In a large skillet over medium-high heat, heat the oil.

3. **Cook the cod.** Add the seasoned cod to the skillet and cook for 4 to 5 minutes per side, until it flakes easily with a fork.

4. **Prepare the salsa.** While the cod cooks, in a medium bowl, stir together the corn, jalapeño, onion, cilantro, lime juice, cumin, and salt.

5. **Finish.** Serve the cod topped with the salsa.

Per Serving: Calories: 234; Saturated Fat: 1g; Total Fat: 10g; Protein: 23g; Total Carbs: 18g; Fiber: 4g; Sodium: 540mg

SHRIMP TABBOULEH

SERVES: 4 | PREP TIME: 10 minutes COOK TIME: 15 minutes

This is a delicious light meal! Traditional tabbouleh is made with bulgur, which typically takes about 20 minutes to cook. In this recipe I use couscous instead. Couscous is very quick and hands-off, so you can focus on prepping and cooking the rest of the ingredients. This Shrimp Tabbouleh's fresh taste comes from the lemon juice, parsley, and mint.

For the dressing

¼ cup olive oil

¼ cup freshly squeezed lemon juice

½ cup chopped fresh parsley

¼ cup chopped fresh mint

2 scallions, chopped

½ teaspoon salt

½ teaspoon freshly ground black pepper

For the tabbouleh

1½ cups water

1 cup couscous

1 tablespoon olive oil

1 pound (16 to 20 count) raw peeled and deveined shrimp

1 garlic clove, minced

1 pint cherry tomatoes, halved

½ cup crumbled feta cheese

4 cups fresh arugula or mixed greens

1. **Prepare the dressing.** In a small bowl, whisk the oil, lemon juice, parsley, mint, scallions, salt, and pepper until combined. Set aside.

2. **Cook the couscous.** In a medium pot over high heat, bring the water to a boil. Add the couscous, cover the pot, and remove it from the heat. Let sit for 5 minutes, or until you are ready to use it. Fluff it with a fork before using.

3. **Cook the shrimp.** In a large skillet over medium-high heat, heat the oil. Add the shrimp and cook for 3 to 5 minutes, or until pink, turning once about halfway through the cooking time. Add the garlic and cook for 1 minute more. Set aside.

4. **Combine the tabbouleh components.** In a large bowl, combine the cooked couscous, cooked shrimp, tomatoes, and dressing. Stir well to combine.

5. **Add the cheese.** Top with the feta cheese.

6. **Finish.** Serve over the arugula or greens.

Per Serving: Calories: 494; Saturated Fat: 6g; Total Fat: 23g; Protein: 33g; Total Carbs: 41g; Fiber: 5g; Sodium: 665mg

GARLIC ROASTED COD WITH TOMATOES AND BEANS

SERVES: 4 | PREP TIME: 10 minutes COOK TIME: 20 minutes |

This roasted cod is about to become your go-to dinner for company. The ingredients are simple, but the end result is super flavorful and beyond impressive. I mean, roasted tomatoes, white beans, shallots, garlic, and fresh thyme? Yes, you're fancy.

1 cup cherry tomatoes, halved

2 shallots, diced

1 (14-ounce) can white beans, rinsed and drained

4 garlic cloves, minced, divided

2 tablespoons olive oil

Salt

Freshly ground black pepper

4 (6-ounce) cod fillets

2 tablespoons butter, melted

2 teaspoons fresh thyme leaves

1. **Preheat the oven.** Preheat the oven to 450°F.

2. **Prepare the tomato and bean mixture.** In a 9-by-13-inch baking dish, combine the tomatoes, shallots, beans, and half of the garlic. Drizzle with the oil and toss to combine. Season the mixture with salt and pepper.

3. **Prepare the cod.** Place the cod on top of the tomato-bean mixture. Top with the remaining minced garlic and brush the cod with the melted butter. Season the cod with salt and pepper.

4. **Bake the cod.** Bake for 20 minutes, or until the fish is opaque and flakes easily with a fork.

5. **Finish.** Serve topped with the thyme.

Make It Healthier: Use olive oil instead of butter for a dish that is lower in saturated fat.

Serving Tip: While the cod bakes, you can prepare a simple side salad, such as the Strawberry Avocado Salad (page 33) and cut up a loaf of fresh bread to serve alongside, if you like.

Per Serving: Calories: 401; Saturated Fat: 5g; Total Fat: 15g; Protein: 39g; Total Carbs: 30g; Fiber: 11g; Sodium: 188mg

GRILLED HALIBUT WITH JALAPEÑO CITRUS SALSA

SERVES: 4 to 6 | **PREP TIME:** 15 minutes **COOK TIME:** 10 minutes

Halibut is an oily whitefish that is full of omega-3 fatty acids and makes a great addition to a healthy diet. In this recipe the halibut steaks are quickly marinated in a fresh orange and garlic mixture, then topped with a spicy citrus salsa that will really wow your dinner guests!

For the halibut

2 tablespoons olive oil

1 tablespoon freshly
  squeezed orange juice

2 garlic cloves, minced

½ teaspoon salt

4 to 6 halibut steaks

For the salsa

1 navel orange, sectioned
  and diced

1 Cara Cara orange,
  sectioned and diced

1 blood orange, sectioned
  and diced

1 jalapeño pepper, seeded,
  and diced

¼ red onion, diced

¼ cup chopped fresh
  cilantro

Juice of 1 lime

½ teaspoon salt

1. **Prepare the halibut.** In a small bowl, whisk the oil, orange juice, garlic, and salt until combined. Place the halibut steaks in a baking dish and drizzle with the marinade. Let sit for about 10 minutes.

2. **Prepare the salsa.** While the halibut marinates, make the salsa. In a medium bowl, stir together the oranges, jalapeño, onion, cilantro, lime juice, and salt. Set aside.

3. **Preheat the grill.** Preheat the grill to medium-high heat, or place a grill pan over medium-high heat on the stovetop.

4. **Grill the halibut.** Place the halibut on the grill and grill for 4 to 5 minutes per side, or until cooked through and the fish flakes easily with a fork.

5. **Finish.** Serve the halibut topped with the salsa.

Make It Faster: Use a large can of mandarin oranges instead of the fresh oranges to reduce prep time.

Serving Tip: Serve this dish alongside grilled or Pan-Sautéed Vegetables (page 140) and a loaf of fresh bread.

Per Serving: Calories: 256; Saturated Fat: 1g; Total Fat: 10g; Protein: 25g; Total Carbs: 18g; Fiber: 4g; Sodium: 641mg

SHRIMP BURRITO BOWLS WITH AVOCADO SALSA

SERVES: 4 to 6 | **PREP TIME:** 15 minutes **COOK TIME:** 10 minutes

Burrito bowls are one of our favorite go-to weeknight meals. (Who needs fast-casual restaurants?) My husband loves to shove all the ingredients into a huge tortilla, but my boys and I prefer eating them in true bowl fashion. These Shrimp Burrito Bowls come together quickly with shrimp and a fresh avocado salsa!

For the burrito bowls

1½ cups rice

3 cups water

1 tablespoon olive oil

1½ pounds (16 to 20 count) raw peeled and deveined shrimp

2 teaspoons chili powder

1 teaspoon ground cumin

½ teaspoon garlic powder

½ teaspoon cayenne pepper

1 (16-ounce) can black beans, rinsed and drained

For the avocado salsa

2 cups frozen corn, thawed

2 scallions, chopped

1 avocado, peeled, pitted, and diced

1 jalapeño pepper, stemmed, seeded, and diced

Juice of 1 lime

¼ cup chopped fresh cilantro

1. **Cook the rice.** In a medium saucepan, bring the rice and water to a boil over high heat. Reduce the heat to low, cover the pan, and simmer the rice for 15 to 18 minutes, or until the water is absorbed and the rice is tender.

2. **Cook the shrimp.** While the rice cooks, heat the oil in a large skillet over medium-high heat. Add the shrimp, chili powder, cumin, garlic powder, and cayenne. Cook for 3 to 4 minutes, or until the shrimp are pink, turning once about halfway through the cooking time. Set aside.

3. **Prepare the avocado salsa.** In a medium bowl, stir together the corn, scallions, avocado, jalapeño, lime juice, and cilantro. Set aside.

4. **Finish.** Ladle the rice into bowls and top with the shrimp, beans, and salsa.

Make It Healthier: Use quinoa instead of rice for a more nutritious burrito bowl base.

Per Serving: Calories: 733; Saturated Fat: 2g; Total Fat: 14g; Protein: 53g; Total Carbs: 103g; Fiber: 17g; Sodium: 230mg

COCONUT CURRY MUSSELS

SERVES: 4 | **PREP TIME:** 15 minutes **COOK TIME:** 12 minutes

Mussels always remind me of my brief time living in Seattle, as that was the first place I cooked them myself. I was a little intimidated, but after making them and realizing how simple it really was, I was hooked. I love finding mussels on menus, especially when they are served with grilled bread or fries, but I honestly love making them at home even more because of this coconut curry sauce—I'm not lying when I say I could drink this sauce.

2½ to 3 pounds mussels
2 tablespoons coconut oil
½ red onion, sliced
1 red bell pepper, seeded
  and sliced
2 garlic cloves, minced
1 teaspoon minced peeled
  fresh ginger
¼ cup red curry paste
1 (14-ounce) can
  coconut milk
Juice of 1 lime, for topping
Chopped fresh cilantro,
  for topping

1. **Prepare the mussels.** Place the mussels in a large bowl of cold water. Scrub them clean and remove the beards.

2. **Prepare the sauce.** In a large saucepan over medium heat, heat the coconut oil. Add the onion and bell pepper and cook for about 5 minutes, or until softened. Stir in the garlic and ginger and cook for 1 minute more. Add the curry paste and coconut milk and bring to a simmer.

3. **Cook the mussels.** Add the mussels to the pan, cover, and cook for 4 to 5 minutes, or until the mussels have opened. Discard any mussels that do not open.

4. **Finish.** Serve topped with a squeeze of lime juice and a sprinkle of cilantro.

Serving Tip: I highly recommend serving these with crusty grilled bread or French fries. Hey, a French fry every now and then is a beautiful thing in my book!

Per Serving: Calories: 581; Saturated Fat: 29g; Total Fat: 41g; Protein: 33g; Total Carbs: 22g; Fiber: 3g; Sodium: 1,529mg

SWEET AND SOUR SHRIMP STIR-FRY

SERVES: 4 to 6 | PREP TIME: 10 minutes COOK TIME: 20 minutes

Who needs takeout when you can make your own stir-fry faster than it could be delivered to your door? This Sweet and Sour Shrimp Stir-Fry is also much healthier.

For the stir-fry

1½ cups rice, or 8 ounces rice noodles

3 cups water

2 tablespoons canola oil

1 pound (16 to 20 count) raw peeled and deveined shrimp

2 cups chopped broccoli florets

2 carrots, peeled and diced

1 red bell pepper, seeded and sliced

For the sauce

½ cup honey

⅓ cup rice vinegar

⅓ cup pineapple juice

2 tablespoons soy sauce

1 tablespoon Sriracha

½ teaspoon garlic powder

1 tablespoon cornstarch

1 tablespoon water

1. **Cook the rice.** In a medium saucepan, bring the rice and water to a boil over high heat. Reduce the heat to low, cover the pan, and simmer the rice for 15 to 18 minutes, or until the water is absorbed and the rice is tender. If using rice noodles, cook them according to the directions on the package.

2. **Cook the shrimp.** While the rice cooks, heat the oil in a large wok or skillet over medium-high heat. Add the shrimp and cook for 3 to 5 minutes, or until pink, turning once about halfway through the cooking time. Remove the shrimp from the skillet and transfer to a plate.

3. **Cook the vegetables.** Return the skillet to the heat and add the broccoli, carrots, and bell pepper. Cook for 5 to 7 minutes, or until softened.

4. **Prepare the sauce.** While the veggies cook, whisk the honey, vinegar, pineapple juice, soy sauce, Sriracha, and garlic powder together in a medium bowl. In a small bowl, whisk the cornstarch and water until the cornstarch dissolves. Whisk this slurry into the honey-vinegar mixture until combined.

5. **Combine the vegetables and shrimp.** Once the veggies are cooked, return the shrimp to the pan along with the sauce. Mix well to incorporate the sauce into the veggies and shrimp and cook for 1 to 2 minutes, or until the sauce thickens.

6. **Finish.** Serve over the rice and enjoy!

Make It Faster: Buy a bag of chopped broccoli to reduce your prep time.

Make It Healthier: You can also serve this dish with zucchini noodles or cauliflower rice.

Per Serving: Calories: 623; Saturated Fat: 1g; Total Fat: 9g; Protein: 31g; Total Carbs: 105g; Fiber: 4g; Sodium: 650mg

CHIMICHURRI SALMON AND VEGETABLES

SERVES: 4 | PREP TIME: 10 minutes COOK TIME: 20 minutes

Chimichurri is one of my favorite sauces to add to a protein. In this dish, I add it to both the salmon and the vegetables—that's how much I love it. Chimichurri is an oil-based sauce from Argentina and is traditionally made with only parsley, but I love adding fresh cilantro. This dish is bursting with fresh flavor and, I promise you, you will want to put this sauce on everything.

Nonstick cooking spray

For the chimichurri

¾ cup fresh parsley
¾ cup fresh cilantro
¼ white onion
2 garlic cloves, peeled
½ cup olive oil
2 tablespoons red
   wine vinegar
½ teaspoon salt
¼ teaspoon red
   pepper flakes

For the salmon and vegetables

4 (6-ounce) salmon fillets
2 tablespoons olive oil
1 large zucchini, diced
1 summer squash, diced
8 ounces sliced mushrooms

1. **Preheat the oven and prepare the baking sheet.** Preheat the oven to 425°F. Coat a baking sheet with cooking spray.

2. **Prepare the chimichurri.** While the oven preheats, combine the parsley, cilantro, onion, garlic, oil, vinegar, salt, and red pepper flakes in a small food processor. Pulse until well combined. Set aside.

3. **Prepare the salmon.** Place the salmon on the prepared baking sheet and brush each fillet with about 1 tablespoon of the chimichurri.

4. **Bake the salmon.** Bake the salmon for 12 to 15 minutes, or until it flakes easily with a fork.

5. **Cook the vegetables.** While the salmon cooks, heat the oil in a large skillet over medium-high heat. Add the zucchini, squash, mushrooms, and 1 to 2 tablespoons of chimichurri. Cook for about 10 minutes, or until the vegetables are softened.

6. **Finish.** Serve the salmon topped with additional chimichurri, as desired, alongside the vegetables.

Simple Swap: You can swap out the squash and mushrooms for any vegetables you might have on hand! Bell peppers, snow peas, broccoli, and onions are all great options.

Per Serving: Calories: 643; Saturated Fat: 9g; Total Fat: 48g; Protein: 40g; Total Carbs: 9g; Fiber: 3g; Sodium: 433mg

AHI TUNA POKE RICE BOWLS

SERVES: 4 to 6 | **PREP TIME:** 10 minutes **COOK TIME:** 20 minutes

Poke bowls have been all the rage lately, and it's really no surprise. The only cooking involved in these bowls is the rice, as the tuna stays raw, making these super easy to whip up any night of the week. Because the tuna stays raw, though, it's important to find sushi-grade tuna for these bowls—you don't want to shortcut that one.

1½ cups rice

3 cups water

1 pound sushi-grade ahi tuna, cut into ½-inch cubes

2 scallions, chopped

1 tablespoon soy sauce

1 teaspoon sesame oil

½ cucumber, thinly sliced

1 avocado, peeled, pitted, and sliced

1 cup cooked shelled edamame

Chopped scallions, for topping

Sesame seeds, for topping

Sriracha, for topping

1. **Marinate the tuna.** In a medium bowl, stir together the tuna, scallions, soy sauce, and oil. Set aside.

2. **Cook the rice.** In a medium saucepan, bring the rice and water to a boil over high heat. Reduce the heat to low, cover the pan, and simmer the rice for 15 to 18 minutes, or until the water is absorbed and the rice is tender.

3. **Assemble the bowls.** Assemble the bowls by layering the cooked rice, cucumber, avocado, edamame, and tuna.

4. **Finish.** Top with the scallions, sesame seeds, and a drizzle of Sriracha.

Per Serving: Calories: 552; Saturated Fat: 2g; Total Fat: 13g; Protein: 38g; Total Carbs: 69g; Fiber: 6g; Sodium: 387mg

CHAPTER SEVEN
POULTRY

There is no such thing as a boring chicken breast in this chapter. Whereas others might see poultry as flavorless, I see an opportunity to add flavor and have fun. Recipes such as Broccoli Cheddar Chicken Gnocchi (page 103), Coconut Tandoori Chicken (page 106) and Grilled Harissa Chicken and Vegetable Kebabs (page 107) will have you wondering why chicken ever got a bad rep in the first place. There are fun turkey recipes as well, such as One-Skillet Turkey Enchilada Quinoa (page 109) and Turkey Sausage–Stuffed Zucchini Boats (page 113) for easy crowd-pleasing meals.

CREAMY CHICKEN SAUSAGE PESTO PASTA

SERVES: 4 to 6 | **PREP TIME:** 5 minutes **COOK TIME:** 20 minutes |

Using precooked chicken sausage (as opposed to raw chicken) cuts way down on the cooking time in this dish. I love pesto on its own, but when combined with a little half-and-half and mozzarella cheese, it makes a creamy pesto dream!

1 tablespoon olive oil

1 (12-ounce) package chicken sausage, cut into bite-size pieces

8 ounces penne or rigatoni pasta

2 cups chicken broth

⅓ cup jarred pesto

2 cups chopped fresh baby spinach leaves

½ cup half-and-half

1 cup shredded mozzarella cheese

Salt

Freshly ground black pepper

½ cup shredded Parmesan cheese

Chopped fresh basil, for topping

1. **Prepare the skillet.** In a large pot over medium-high heat, heat the oil.

2. **Cook the chicken sausage.** Add the chicken sausage and cook for 3 to 5 minutes, or until it has browned.

3. **Add the pasta.** Stir in the pasta, broth, and pesto.

4. **Cook the pasta.** Bring the mixture to a boil, reduce the heat to a simmer, and cover the pot. Cook for 8 to 10 minutes, or until the pasta is cooked to your desired firmness.

5. **Add additional ingredients.** Stir in the spinach, half-and-half, and mozzarella.

6. **Finish.** Taste and season with salt and pepper. Top with the Parmesan cheese and basil.

Make It Yourself: If you prefer, make your own Pesto (page 137).

Per Serving: Calories: 665; Saturated Fat: 13g; Total Fat: 34g; Protein: 35g; Total Carbs: 53g; Fiber: 2g; Sodium: 1,179mg

ONE-SKILLET CASHEW CHICKEN

SERVES: 4 | PREP TIME: 10 minutes COOK TIME: 20 minutes |

We recently moved and are now in what we call an "Asian Food Dead Zone." As a result, I've really upped my efforts to recreate our favorite dishes at home. This cashew chicken is saucy, crunchy, and so full of flavor. As a bonus, this dish is also healthier than what we'd be eating out anyway.

1½ cups rice

3 cups water

1 tablespoon canola oil

1 pound boneless skinless chicken breasts, cut into 1-inch pieces

1¼ cups chicken broth

⅓ cup soy sauce

3 tablespoons rice vinegar

2 tablespoons brown sugar

4 garlic cloves, minced

1 teaspoon minced peeled fresh ginger

1 teaspoon sesame oil

2 tablespoons cornstarch

1 cup cashews

2 scallions, chopped

1. **Cook the rice.** In a medium saucepan, bring the rice and water to a boil over high heat. Reduce the heat to low, cover the pan, and simmer the rice for 15 to 18 minutes, or until the water is absorbed and the rice is tender.

2. **Cook the chicken.** While the rice cooks, heat the canola oil in a large skillet over medium-high heat. Add the chicken and cook for about 5 minutes, or until it is golden brown and cooked through.

3. **Prepare the sauce.** While the chicken cooks, whisk the broth, soy sauce, vinegar, brown sugar, garlic, ginger, sesame oil, and cornstarch together in a small bowl until the cornstarch dissolves.

4. **Add the sauce.** Once the chicken is done, add the sauce to the chicken. Cook for 2 to 3 minutes, or until it thickens.

5. **Add the cashews.** Add the cashews to the skillet and stir to combine.

6. **Finish.** Serve over the cooked rice, topped with the scallions.

Make It Healthier: Serve with cauliflower rice instead of white rice to cut down on the carbohydrates.

Per Serving: Calories: 664; Saturated Fat: 3g; Total Fat: 22g; Protein: 37g; Total Carbs: 77g; Fiber: 2g; Sodium: 1,505mg

BROCCOLI CHEDDAR CHICKEN GNOCCHI

SERVES: 4 | PREP TIME: 10 minutes COOK TIME: 15 minutes |

My four-year-old is obsessed with Panera's broccoli Cheddar soup, but I can only tolerate it so many times in a week. I've become creative with the ways I serve his favorite soup flavors, and this is his all-time favorite. The cheesy sauce is so simple and creamy, and I love seeing my kids gobble down all the broccoli.

1 (16-ounce) package potato gnocchi (refrigerated or shelf-stable)

2 tablespoons olive oil

1 pound boneless skinless chicken breasts, cut into bite-size pieces

1 head broccoli, chopped into small florets (about 2 cups)

2 tablespoons water

3 tablespoons butter

2 garlic cloves, minced

2 tablespoons all-purpose flour

1½ cups milk

½ teaspoon salt

2 cups shredded Cheddar cheese

1. **Cook the gnocchi.** Cook the gnocchi according to package directions, then drain. While the water heats and the gnocchi cooks, prepare the rest of the dish.

2. **Prepare the skillet.** In a large skillet over medium-high heat, heat the oil.

3. **Cook the chicken.** Add the chicken and cook for about 5 minutes, or until it is golden brown and cooked through.

4. **Steam the broccoli.** While the chicken cooks, place the broccoli in a microwave-safe bowl with the water. Cover with a paper towel and cook on high power for 2 to 3 minutes, or until steamed.

5. **Prepare the cheese sauce.** Remove the chicken from the skillet. Add the butter to the skillet to melt. Add the garlic and cook for 1 minute. Add the flour, whisking to combine with the butter and garlic. Slowly whisk in the milk to combine it with the flour mixture. Stir in the salt and cheese, mixing until the cheese melts.

6. **Finish.** Add the cooked gnocchi, chicken, and broccoli to the cheese sauce and gently stir to coat and combine.

Make It Faster: Use a bag of pre-chopped broccoli to reduce prep time.

Per Serving: Calories: 724; Saturated Fat: 20g; Total Fat: 40g; Protein: 45g; Total Carbs: 44g; Fiber: 3g; Sodium: 1,463mg

HONEY-BALSAMIC CHICKEN THIGHS

SERVES: 4 to 6 | PREP TIME: 5 minutes COOK TIME: 20 minutes

Trying to save money? Chicken thighs are a great economical choice for weeknight cooking. And they're delicious. In this recipe they get tossed in a simple, sweet, and tangy honey-balsamic mixture and are roasted in the oven to crispy perfection.

2 pounds bone-in skin-on chicken thighs

⅓ cup honey

2 tablespoons balsamic vinegar

1 tablespoon olive oil

2 garlic cloves, minced

½ teaspoon salt

1. **Preheat the oven.** Preheat the oven to 425°F.

2. **Prepare the chicken thighs.** Place the chicken thighs in a baking dish.

3. **Prepare the sauce.** In a small bowl, whisk the honey, vinegar, oil, garlic, and salt until combined.

4. **Add the sauce to the chicken.** Drizzle the sauce over the chicken thighs and use a pastry brush to cover them completely.

5. **Finish.** Bake for 20 minutes, or until the chicken is cooked through and reaches an internal temperature of 165°F on an instant-read thermometer.

Serving Tip: While the chicken cooks, prepare a simple side dish, such as Pan-Sautéed Vegetables (page 140).

Per Serving: Calories: 654; Saturated Fat: 16g; Total Fat: 46g; Protein: 38g; Total Carbs: 24g; Fiber: 0g; Sodium: 451mg

CAJUN CHICKEN PASTA

SERVES: 4 | PREP TIME: 10 minutes COOK TIME: 15 minutes |

I had never cooked with Cajun seasoning until I met my husband. He loves anything that I make with it, especially this Cajun Chicken Pasta. I love it, too, because it only uses one pot. It's a winner chicken dinner for us both!

2 tablespoons olive oil

1 pound boneless skinless chicken breasts, cut into strips

2 tablespoons Cajun seasoning

8 ounces penne pasta

1 (15-ounce) can diced tomatoes

1½ cups chicken broth

3 cups fresh baby spinach leaves

½ cup heavy (whipping) cream

1. **Prepare the pot.** In a large pot over medium-high heat, heat the oil.

2. **Cook the chicken.** Add the chicken strips and Cajun seasoning, stir to coat, and cook until the chicken is browned, about 5 minutes; it does not need to be quite cooked through.

3. **Cook the pasta.** Add the pasta, tomatoes, and broth to the pot. Bring to a boil, reduce the heat to maintain a simmer, and cook, uncovered for 8 to 10 minutes, or until the pasta is cooked and liquid is absorbed.

4. **Finish.** Stir in the spinach and heavy cream. Cook, stirring, until the spinach is wilted, 1 to 2 minutes.

Make It Healthier: To cut down on the fat and calories from the heavy cream, use milk instead.

Per Serving: Calories: 528; Saturated Fat: 8g; Total Fat: 22g; Protein: 35g; Total Carbs: 46g; Fiber: 3g; Sodium: 453mg

COCONUT TANDOORI CHICKEN

SERVES: 4 | PREP TIME: 5 minutes COOK TIME: 20 minutes

Indian food is one of my favorite cuisines to make at home, so I just couldn't help but include one of my favorite Indian chicken dishes in this cookbook. The variety of spices in this tandoori chicken is unbeatable, and I love the creaminess from the coconut milk. I use chicken thighs in this dish, which always result in a tender chicken dish.

1½ cups rice

3 cups water

2 tablespoons olive oil

1½ pounds chicken thighs, cut into bite-size pieces

1 tablespoon minced peeled fresh ginger

1 tablespoon curry powder

1 tablespoon ground cumin

1 teaspoon garlic powder

1 teaspoon ground turmeric

1 teaspoon paprika

½ teaspoon chili powder

¼ teaspoon cayenne pepper

½ teaspoon salt

1 (14-ounce) can coconut milk

Fresh cilantro, for topping

1. **Cook the rice.** In a medium saucepan, bring the rice and water to a boil over high heat. Reduce the heat to low, cover the pan, and simmer the rice for 15 to 18 minutes, or until the water is absorbed and the rice is tender.

2. **Prepare the skillet.** In a large skillet over medium-high heat, heat the oil.

3. **Cook the chicken.** Add the chicken and cook for about 5 minutes, or until golden and cooked through.

4. **Add the spices.** Stir in the ginger, curry powder, cumin, garlic powder, turmeric, paprika, chili powder, cayenne, and salt.

5. **Add the coconut milk.** Add the coconut milk, stirring to combine. Bring the mixture to a boil and cook for 2 to 3 minutes.

6. **Finish.** Serve over the cooked rice, topped with the cilantro.

Per Serving: Calories: 920; Saturated Fat: 30g; Total Fat: 57g; Protein: 38g; Total Carbs: 64g; Fiber: 4g; Sodium: 444mg

GRILLED HARISSA CHICKEN AND VEGETABLE KEBABS

SERVES: 4 | **PREP TIME:** 12 minutes **COOK TIME:** 15 minutes |

Harissa is a North African hot chile pepper paste that packs a punch, and I especially love to use it during grilling season. In this recipe, cubes of chicken and fresh vegetables are threaded onto skewers and grilled, so your entire meal can be cooked at once!

½ cup harissa, divided

1¼ pounds boneless skinless chicken breasts, cut into 1-inch pieces

1 red bell pepper, seeded and cut into 1-inch pieces

1 zucchini, cut into ¼-inch slices

1 cup cherry tomatoes

1. **Preheat the grill.** Preheat the grill to medium-high heat.

2. **Prepare the chicken.** In a large bowl, stir together ¼ cup of the harissa and the chicken until well coated.

3. **Thread the chicken and vegetables onto skewers.** Thread the chicken onto skewers, alternating with the bell pepper, zucchini, and tomatoes. The number of skewers this makes will depend on how long they are.

4. **Grill the chicken and vegetables.** Place the skewers on the grill rack and cook for 12 to 15 minutes, or until the chicken is cooked through and the vegetables are tender. Turn the skewers 2 or 3 times while cooking.

5. **Finish.** Brush the skewers with the remaining ¼ cup of harissa.

Serving Tip: If you want to bulk up the meal a little, brush a loaf of bread with olive oil and throw it on the grill for a couple of minutes to serve with this dish.

Per Serving: Calories: 285; Saturated Fat: 0g; Total Fat: 9g; Protein: 33g; Total Carbs: 18g; Fiber: 2g; Sodium: 439mg

THAI PEANUT RAMEN NOODLES

SERVES: 4 | **PREP TIME:** 10 minutes **COOK TIME:** 18 minutes

These ramen noodles are NOT the ones you made in college. The sauce is full of flavor from sweet chili sauce, peanut butter, and coconut milk, and is easily made in the food processor. These slurpable noodles will be a favorite at your family's dinner table!

5 tablespoons olive oil, divided

2 boneless skinless chicken breasts, cut into strips

½ cup peanut butter

¼ cup soy sauce

¼ cup sweet chili sauce

Juice of 1 lime

1 red bell pepper, seeded and diced

½ white onion, diced

1 tablespoon finely chopped peeled fresh ginger

2 garlic cloves, minced

1 (15-ounce) can full-fat coconut milk

2 (3-ounce) packages ramen noodles, seasoning packets discarded

Chopped fresh cilantro, for topping

Chopped scallions, for topping

Chopped peanuts, for topping

1. **Prepare the skillet.** In a large skillet over medium-high heat, heat 1 tablespoon of oil.

2. **Cook the chicken.** Add the chicken and cook for about 5 minutes, or until cooked through.

3. **Prepare the sauce.** While the chicken cooks, combine the peanut butter, soy sauce, chili sauce, lime juice, and 2 tablespoons of the oil in a small food processor. Pulse to combine until smooth.

4. **Cook the vegetables.** Add the remaining 2 tablespoons of oil, the pepper, and the onion to the skillet with the chicken and cook for 5 minutes, or until they are softened. Stir in the ginger and garlic and cook for 1 minute more.

5. **Combine and cook the noodles.** Add the sauce from the food processor along with the coconut milk, stirring to combine. Add the ramen noodles, nestling them into the sauce. Cover the skillet and cook for 3 to 4 minutes, or until the noodles are cooked through.

6. **Finish.** Serve topped with the cilantro, scallions, and peanuts.

Per Serving: Calories: 848; Saturated Fat: 31g; Total Fat: 69g; Protein: 34g; Total Carbs: 32g; Fiber: 6g; Sodium: 1,393mg

ONE-SKILLET TURKEY ENCHILADA QUINOA

SERVES: 4 to 6 | **PREP TIME:** 7 minutes **COOK TIME:** 23 minutes |

Ground turkey, quinoa, black beans, corn, and enchilada sauce are combined in this one-skillet, family-pleasing dinner. This is one great example of a dinner that can be flavorful, yet easy to make. The generous dose of cheese on top doesn't hurt, either!

1 cup quinoa, rinsed well

2 cups water

1 tablespoon olive oil

1 pound ground turkey

1 (16-ounce) can black beans, rinsed and drained

1 (10-ounce) can enchilada sauce

1 cup frozen corn

3 scallions, chopped

1 teaspoon ground cumin

½ teaspoon salt

1 cup shredded Cheddar cheese

Fresh cilantro, for topping

1. **Preheat the oven.** Preheat the oven to 425°F.

2. **Cook the quinoa.** In a medium pot, combine the quinoa and water. Bring to a boil, reduce the heat, cover the pot, and simmer for 15 to 18 minutes, or until the quinoa is cooked and the water is absorbed.

3. **Prepare the skillet.** While the quinoa cooks, heat the oil in an ovenproof skillet over medium-high heat.

4. **Cook the ground turkey.** Add the ground turkey and cook for 5 to 7 minutes, breaking it into smaller pieces with the back of a wooden spoon as it cooks, until it is no longer pink.

5. **Add the remaining ingredients.** Add the cooked quinoa, beans, enchilada sauce, corn, scallions, cumin, and salt to the skillet and mix well to combine. Top with the cheese.

6. **Bake.** Bake for 5 minutes, or until the cheese melts.

7. **Finish.** Serve topped with the cilantro.

Per Serving: Calories: 628; Saturated Fat: 10g; Total Fat: 27g; Protein: 41g; Total Carbs: 56g; Fiber: 11g; Sodium: 765mg

ONE-POT GREEK CHICKEN AND RICE

SERVES: 4 to 6 | PREP TIME: 7 minutes COOK TIME: 23 minutes |

In general, I can tell before a meal whether my husband will absolutely love it or if he will just eat it. I predicted this Greek chicken and rice would be one he would appreciate, but not rave over. Boy, was I wrong! He could not get enough of this dish (sans olives!), and I felt the same way (with olives!). This chicken and rice dish is full of flavor from the dried herbs and lemon zest, and could not be easier to prepare.

2 tablespoons olive oil

2 boneless skinless chicken breasts, cut into 1-inch pieces

2 cups chicken broth

1 cup rice

2 tablespoons freshly squeezed lemon juice

2 teaspoons lemon zest

1 teaspoon dried oregano

1 teaspoon dried rosemary

1 teaspoon dried thyme

½ teaspoon salt

1 cup cherry tomatoes, quartered

1 cup crumbled feta cheese

½ cup Kalamata olives

Chopped fresh parsley, for topping

1. **Prepare the skillet.** In a large skillet over medium-high heat, heat the oil.

2. **Cook the chicken.** Add the chicken and cook for 3 to 5 minutes, or until golden brown; it does not need to be cooked through at this point.

3. **Add the seasonings.** Stir in the broth, rice, lemon juice, lemon zest, oregano, rosemary, thyme, and salt.

4. **Cook the rice.** Bring the mixture to a boil, reduce the heat to maintain a simmer, and cover the skillet. Cook for 15 to 17 minutes, or until the broth is absorbed and the rice is cooked.

5. **Finish.** Top with the tomatoes, feta cheese, olives, and parsley.

Make It Faster: This would be a great recipe to use up leftover Perfect Whole Roasted Chicken (page 144).

Per Serving: Calories: 635; Saturated Fat: 7g; Total Fat: 24g; Protein: 59g; Total Carbs: 43g; Fiber: 2g; Sodium: 1,358mg

ONE-PAN DIJON HERB CHICKEN AND VEGETABLES

SERVES: 4 to 6 | **PREP TIME:** 10 minutes **COOK TIME:** 20 minutes |

I'm a sucker for any meal that can be made in one vessel—the fewer dishes, the better! We went through a period of not having a dishwasher after ours broke while I was developing this cookbook. Needless to say, one-dish meals were definitely a priority. I love the fact that this dish is so simple, yet it is still full of flavor.

1 pound boneless skinless chicken breasts, cut into bite-size pieces

2 cups chopped broccolini

1 red bell pepper, seeded and sliced

1 red onion, cut into large chunks

8 ounces button mushrooms, sliced

⅓ cup olive oil

1 tablespoon Dijon mustard

1 teaspoon Italian seasoning

3 garlic cloves, minced

Salt

Freshly ground black pepper

1. **Preheat the oven and prepare the baking sheets.** Preheat the oven to 425°F. Line two baking sheets with aluminum foil.

2. **Prepare the vegetables and chicken.** While the oven preheats, evenly divide the chicken, broccolini, bell pepper, onion, and mushrooms between the prepared baking sheets, spreading them out.

3. **Prepare the dressing.** In a Mason jar, combine the oil, mustard, Italian seasoning, and garlic, and season with salt and pepper. Put the lid on the jar and shake until the dressing is well combined.

4. **Combine the dressing with the vegetables and chicken.** Drizzle the dressing evenly over the two baking sheets and, using a spoon or your hands, toss until the veggies and chicken are coated.

5. **Finish.** Roast the chicken and vegetables for 20 minutes, stirring and rotating the pans after 10 minutes.

Make It Faster: Buy sliced mushrooms to reduce the prep time.

Per Serving: Calories: 321; Saturated Fat: 3g; Total Fat: 20g; Protein: 27g; Total Carbs: 9g; Fiber: 2g; Sodium: 115mg

CHEESY ASPARAGUS AND PROSCIUTTO-STUFFED CHICKEN BREASTS

SERVES: 4 | PREP TIME: 10 minutes COOK TIME: 20 minutes

This chicken is easy enough for a weeknight but impressive enough for a dinner party. I love jazzing up chicken breasts by stuffing them, and this combination of fresh asparagus, prosciutto, and Gouda cheese is one of my favorites. This dish is best in spring and summer when fresh, in-season asparagus is readily found!

Nonstick cooking spray

4 boneless skinless chicken breast halves

12 asparagus spears, woody ends trimmed

2 ounces thinly sliced prosciutto

½ cup shredded Gouda cheese

½ cup bread crumbs

½ tablespoon Italian seasoning

½ teaspoon salt

1. **Preheat the oven and prepare a baking sheet.** Preheat the oven to 425°F. Line a baking sheet with aluminum foil and coat it with cooking spray.

2. **Prepare the chicken.** Halve each chicken breast lengthwise, not cutting all the way through, creating a pocket that opens like a book.

3. **Stuff the chicken.** Place 3 asparagus spears, 1 slice of the prosciutto, and 2 tablespoons of the Gouda into each pocket. Fold the other half of the chicken back over the top. Repeat with the remaining chicken.

4. **Prepare the bread crumbs.** In a shallow bowl, stir together the bread crumbs, Italian seasoning, and salt.

5. **Dip the chicken.** Dip each chicken breast into the bread crumb mixture, coating each side, and place each one on the prepared baking sheet.

6. **Finish.** Bake for 20 minutes, or until the chicken is golden brown and cooked through and reaches an internal temperature of 165°F.

Serving Tip: While the chicken bakes, cook a side of rice or couscous.

Simple Swap: Use Italian seasoned bread crumbs to reduce the prep and make this a 5-ingredient meal!

Per Serving: Calories: 273; Saturated Fat: 3g; Total Fat: 9g; Protein: 34g; Total Carbs: 13g; Fiber: 2g; Sodium: 735mg

TURKEY SAUSAGE-STUFFED ZUCCHINI BOATS

SERVES: 4 | **PREP TIME:** 10 minutes **COOK TIME:** 20 minutes

This recipe uses the microwave to speed up the cooking process. The zucchini gets nuked for a couple of minutes to soften up, and then the only other cooking time is for the turkey sausage and to melt the cheese on top. These stuffed zucchini boats are delicious, filling, and low in carbs!

4 medium zucchini

2 tablespoons olive oil, divided

1 pound turkey sausage

1 small red onion, diced

1 green bell pepper, seeded and diced

1 (14-ounce) jar pizza sauce

1½ cups shredded mozzarella cheese

1. **Preheat the oven.** Preheat the oven to 450°F.

2. **Prepare the zucchini.** Halve each zucchini horizontally and use a small spoon to scoop out the seeds. If they don't lie flat, trim a thin strip from the bottom. Place them on a microwave-safe plate, brush with 1 tablespoon of the oil, and microwave for 3 to 4 minutes on high power until tender. Transfer the zucchini halves to a sheet pan or a 9-by-13-inch baking dish.

3. **Cook the sausage and vegetables.** While the zucchini is cooking, heat the remaining 1 tablespoon of oil in a large skillet over medium-high heat. Add the sausage, onion, and pepper. Cook for 5 to 7 minutes, breaking the turkey up into smaller pieces with the back of a wooden spoon as it cooks, until browned.

4. **Prepare the zucchini boats.** Spread about 2 tablespoons of pizza sauce in each zucchini boat. Evenly distribute the sausage and the cooked veggies on top of the pizza sauce and top each with mozzarella.

5. **Finish.** Bake for 5 to 10 minutes, or until the cheese melts.

Per Serving: Calories: 504; Saturated Fat: 11g; Total Fat: 31g; Protein: 33g; Total Carbs: 26g; Fiber: 5g; Sodium: 1,372mg

ALMOND-CRUSTED CHICKEN TENDERS AND CREAMY DIJON SAUCE

SERVES: 4 | **PREP TIME:** 12 minutes **COOK TIME:** 18 minutes

The chicken tenders in this recipe are nothing like the ones you'd pick up from a drive-thru—they're fresh, healthy, and tasty. And, best of all, chicken tenders are smaller than breasts and, therefore, require much less cooking time. When dipped in a mixture of bread crumbs and almonds, the chicken tenders are crunchy and delicious. I'm definitely a sauce girl, and this creamy mustard sauce is the perfect tangy accompaniment!

For the chicken tenders

2 large eggs, whisked
½ cup all-purpose flour
⅔ cup whole almonds
1 cup bread crumbs
½ teaspoon dried oregano
½ teaspoon salt
1½ pounds chicken tenders

For the creamy mustard sauce

1 tablespoon butter
2 shallots, diced
1 garlic clove, minced
½ cup heavy (whipping) cream
1 tablespoon Dijon mustard
Salt
Freshly ground black pepper

1. **Preheat the oven and prepare the sheet.** Preheat the oven to 425°F. Line a baking sheet with aluminum foil and set aside.

2. **Prepare the eggs and flour.** Place the eggs in a shallow bowl and place the flour in another shallow bowl.

3. **Prepare the almond coating.** In a small food processor, pulse the almonds until they resembles coarse crumbs. In a third shallow bowl, stir together the bread crumbs, ground almonds, oregano, and salt.

4. **Prepare the chicken.** Dip each chicken tender into the flour, into the egg, and finally into the bread crumb–almond mixture. Place the coated chicken tenders onto the prepared baking sheet.

5. **Bake.** Bake for 15 to 18 minutes, or until golden brown.

6. **Prepare the sauce.** While the chicken cooks, melt the butter in a saucepan over medium heat. Add the shallots and cook for 3 to 5 minutes, or until softened. Stir in the garlic and cook for 1 minute more. Whisk in the heavy cream and mustard until the mixture is creamy. Season with salt and pepper. Simmer for 3 to 5 minutes, or until the sauce thickens.

7. **Finish.** Serve the chicken tenders topped with the creamy mustard sauce.

Make It Healthier: Use whole milk or half-and-half instead of heavy cream to lighten the sauce.

Serving Tip: While the chicken bakes, prepare a side dish of Pan-Sautéed Vegetables (page 140).

Per Serving: Calories: 630; Saturated Fat: 11g; Total Fat: 32g; Protein: 48g; Total Carbs: 37g; Fiber: 4g; Sodium: 688mg

CHAPTER EIGHT
PORK AND BEEF

If you have ever wondered what on Earth you were going to do with another pound of ground beef or package of pork chops, look no further! My Italian Sloppy Joes (page 128) will be a huge hit with your family, and Balsamic-Glazed Pork Chops (page 123) will become a new favorite. I use tricks like parcooking vegetables in the microwave and cutting up a pork loin for kebabs to save time and get dinner on the table faster than ever!

PROSCIUTTO AND FIG FLATBREADS

SERVES: 4 | PREP TIME: 5 minutes COOK TIME: 5 minutes | ⑤

This recipe is for anyone who loves a bit of sweet with their savory. The combination of the sweet fig jam, the salty prosciutto, and the tangy goat cheese is out-of-this-world addictive. Each flatbread will serve two people. I recommend serving with an easy green salad for a more filling meal—you will have plenty of time to whip one up, as these flatbreads only take 10 minutes!

2 large flatbreads or naan

½ cup fig jam or preserves

2 ounces thinly sliced prosciutto

8 ounces crumbled goat cheese

1 cup fresh arugula

1. **Preheat the oven.** Preheat the oven to 400°F.

2. **Prepare the flatbread.** Place each flatbread on a baking sheet. Spread each one with ¼ cup of the fig jam. Top each with the prosciutto and sprinkle with the cheese.

3. **Bake.** Bake for 4 to 5 minutes, or until the cheese is softened and the prosciutto begins to crisp.

4. **Finish.** Top the flatbreads with the arugula.

Smart Shopping: I buy goat cheese in a log and crumble it myself—it's less expensive this way.

Per Serving: Calories: 418; Saturated Fat: 8g; Total Fat: 13g; Protein: 16g; Total Carbs: 50g; Fiber: 1g; Sodium: 619mg

CREAMY SAUSAGE AND SPINACH GNOCCHI

SERVES: 4 to 6 | PREP TIME: 10 minutes COOK TIME: 20 minutes |

It used to be you had to make your own gnocchi from scratch or go to a restaurant to enjoy eating it. These days, we're really spoiled by the options at the grocery store. In this one-skillet dish, the gnocchi is cooked right in the pan with the rest of the ingredients, so it really has a chance to soak up all the flavor. This is a family favorite, especially loved by my boys—but who doesn't love pillowy clouds of pasta goodness?

1 tablespoon olive oil
1 pound Italian sausage
1 small white onion, diced
1 (16-ounce) package potato gnocchi (refrigerated or shelf-stable)
1 (15-ounce) can Italian diced tomatoes
¾ cup chicken broth
½ cup half-and-half
3 cups chopped baby spinach leaves
½ cup shredded Parmesan cheese, plus more for topping

1. **Prepare the skillet.** In a large skillet over medium-high heat, heat the oil.

2. **Cook the sausage and onion.** Add the sausage and onion to the skillet and cook for about 5 minutes, or until the sausage is browned and the onion is softened.

3. **Add the gnocchi, tomatoes, and broth.** Stir in the gnocchi, tomatoes, and broth and bring to a boil. Reduce the heat, cover the skillet, and simmer for 8 to 10 minutes, or until the gnocchi have softened.

4. **Add the half-and-half and spinach.** Stir in the half-and-half and the spinach. Cook, stirring, for 1 to 2 minutes, or until the spinach wilts.

5. **Add the cheese.** Add the cheese and cook, stirring until it melts.

6. **Finish.** Serve topped with additional cheese.

Make It Healthier: Use whole milk instead of half-and-half to lighten the sauce.

Per Serving: Calories: 735; Saturated Fat: 18g; Total Fat: 46g; Protein: 32g; Total Carbs: 47g; Fiber: 2g; Sodium: 1,512mg

TERIYAKI PORK AND PINEAPPLE STIR-FRY

SERVES: 4 to 6 | PREP TIME: 10 minutes COOK TIME: 20 minutes

I'm not one for pineapple on my pizza, but in my stir-fry? Yes, please! This pork and pineapple stir-fry tastes just like something you'd get for takeout, but much healthier. The sweet and savory combination is in full force in this dish and is sure to satisfy that takeout craving!

1½ cups rice

3 cups water

1 tablespoon olive oil

1 red onion, diced

1 red bell pepper, seeded and diced

1½ pounds boneless pork tenderloin, cut into bite-size pieces

1 (12-ounce) can diced pineapple, drained

¾ cup store-bought teriyaki sauce

Chopped scallions, for garnishing

1. **Cook the rice.** In a medium saucepan, bring the rice and water to a boil over high heat. Reduce the heat to low, cover the pan, and simmer the rice for 15 to 18 minutes, or until the water is absorbed and the rice is tender.

2. **Prepare the skillet.** While the rice cooks, heat the oil in a large skillet over medium-high heat.

3. **Cook the onion and bell pepper.** Add the onion and bell pepper and cook for about 5 minutes, or until softened. Remove the onion and pepper from the skillet and set aside.

4. **Cook the pork.** Return the skillet to the heat and add the pork. Cook for 8 to 10 minutes, or until the pork is cooked through.

5. **Add the pineapple and teriyaki.** Stir in the reserved onion and pepper, as well as the pineapple and teriyaki sauce. Cook for 1 to 2 minutes, or until warmed through.

6. **Finish.** Serve over the cooked rice, garnished with scallions.

Make It Faster: Use chopped onions and bell peppers from the produce section, or a frozen stir-fry mix to reduce prep time.

Make It Yourself: If you have extra time, you can make your own Teriyaki Sauce (page 138).

Per Serving: Calories: 576; Saturated Fat: 2g; Total Fat: 9g; Protein: 41g; Total Carbs: 82g; Fiber: 3g; Sodium: 2,407mg

EGG ROLL RICE BOWLS

SERVES: 4 to 6 | **PREP TIME:** 10 minutes **COOK TIME:** 20 minutes

This dish has all the flavors and textures of an egg roll—but in a convenient (unfried) bowl! The pork and cabbage filling is, essentially, what you'd find in any egg roll, and the crunchy wonton strips and sweet Thai chile sauce drizzled on top take it from good to AMAZING.

1½ cups rice

3 cups water

1 pound ground pork

1 tablespoon sesame oil

1 small white onion, diced

1 cup shredded carrot
(about 2 carrots)

4 cups shredded cabbage

3 garlic cloves, minced

¼ cup soy sauce

1 teaspoon ground ginger

Chopped scallions,
for topping

Crispy wonton strips,
for topping

Thai chile sauce,
for topping

1. **Cook the rice.** In a medium saucepan, bring the rice and water to a boil over high heat. Reduce the heat to low, cover the pan, and simmer the rice for 15 to 18 minutes, or until the water is absorbed and the rice is tender.

2. **Cook the pork.** While the rice cooks, in a large skillet over medium heat, cook the pork until browned, breaking it up with the back of a wooden spoon into smaller pieces as it cooks.

3. **Add the sesame oil and vegetables.** Add the oil, onion, carrot, and cabbage. Cook for about 5 minutes, or until the vegetables soften.

4. **Add the garlic, soy sauce, and ginger.** Stir in the garlic, soy sauce, and ginger and cook for 1 minute more.

5. **Finish.** Serve the egg roll mixture over the rice, topped with the scallions and wonton strips and drizzled with the chile sauce.

Love Your Leftovers: Place leftover egg roll filling into a tortilla for lunch the next day.

Make It Faster: Instead of shredding the carrots and cabbage yourself, buy shredded carrots and coleslaw mix.

Per Serving: Calories: 658; Saturated Fat: 8g; Total Fat: 25g; Protein: 29g; Total Carbs: 78g; Fiber: 4g; Sodium: 1,151mg

BALSAMIC-GLAZED PORK CHOPS

SERVES: 4 | **PREP TIME:** 5 minutes **COOK TIME:** 15 minutes

In this recipe, pork chops are simply pan-seared in olive oil and drizzled with a sweet balsamic glaze that adds so much flavor. I always use a meat thermometer when cooking pork, to ensure it is cooked properly. If you don't own one, go get one (it's better to be safe)!

¼ cup balsamic vinegar

2 tablespoons honey

1 tablespoon Dijon mustard

2 garlic cloves, minced

2 tablespoons olive oil

4 (6-ounce) boneless
   pork chops

Salt

Freshly ground
   black pepper

1. **Prepare the balsamic glaze.** In a small saucepan over medium heat, stir together the vinegar, honey, mustard, and garlic. Bring to a simmer and cook the glaze for 5 to 8 minutes, or until the mixture has reduced and coats the back of a spoon.

2. **Cook the pork chops.** While the glaze reduces, heat the oil in a large skillet over medium-high heat. Season the chops on each side with salt and pepper. Add the chops to the skillet and cook for 5 to 6 minutes per side, or until the internal temperature reaches 140°F to 145°F on an instant-read thermometer.

3. **Finish.** Serve the chops drizzled with the balsamic glaze.

Serving Tip: Serve these pork chops with a side of Pan-Sautéed Vegetables (page 140).

Per Serving: Calories: 364; Saturated Fat: 7g; Total Fat: 23g; Protein: 30g; Total Carbs: 11g; Fiber: 0g; Sodium: 613mg

GRILLED ORANGE-GINGER PORK AND VEGETABLE KEBABS

SERVES: 4 | PREP TIME: 15 minutes COOK TIME: 12 minutes

Kebabs are a faster way to grill meat. Cutting the pork into smaller pieces drastically cuts the cooking time. This pork gets a quick marinade in a ginger-orange mixture that is so full of flavor. I love using bell peppers in this recipe, but feel free to mix it up with other vegetables that might be in season. Summer squash, tomatoes, and mushrooms would all be delicious!

For the orange-ginger marinade

Zest of 1 orange

Juice of 1 orange

¼ cup soy sauce

3 tablespoons olive oil

2 tablespoons honey

3 garlic cloves, minced

1 tablespoon minced peeled fresh ginger

For the pork and vegetable kebabs

2 pounds pork loin, cut into 1-inch cubes

1 red bell pepper, seeded and cut into 1-inch pieces

1 yellow bell pepper, seeded and cut into 1-inch pieces

1 red onion, cut into 1-inch pieces

1. **Prepare the marinade.** In a medium bowl, whisk the orange zest, orange juice, soy sauce, oil, honey, garlic, and ginger until combined. Remove 3 tablespoons of the marinade and reserve.

2. **Prepare the pork.** Add the pork to the bowl with the remaining marinade and let sit for 5 minutes.

3. **Preheat the grill.** While the pork marinates, preheat the grill to medium-high heat.

4. **Assemble the kebabs.** Thread the vegetables and pork onto metal skewers, alternating the pork, onion, pepper, until all have been used. Brush the vegetables with the reserved marinade.

5. **Finish.** Grill the skewers for 3 to 4 minutes per side, about 12 minutes total, until cooked through, with an internal temperature of 160°F on an instant-read thermometer.

Serving Tip: Grill slices of bread brushed with olive oil at the same time to serve with the kebabs.

Per Serving: Calories: 510; Saturated Fat: 8g; Total Fat: 27g; Protein: 45g; Total Carbs: 25g; Fiber: 3g; Sodium: 1,704mg

THAI COCONUT CURRY MEATBALLS

SERVES: 4 | PREP TIME: 10 minutes COOK TIME: 20 minutes

If you're a fan of Thai food, you will love these meatballs. These curry-spiced meatballs are oven-baked and combined with a silky coconut milk sauce. Serve them on top of rice, cauliflower rice, or with a side of Pan-Sautéed Vegetables (page 140).

For the meatballs

Nonstick cooking spray

1 pound ground pork

¼ cup bread crumbs

2 garlic cloves, minced

2 teaspoons minced peeled fresh ginger

1 teaspoon curry powder

1 teaspoon salt

1 small white onion, diced, divided

Cooked rice, cauliflower rice, or zucchini noodles, for serving

Fresh cilantro, for garnishing

For the sauce

1 tablespoon coconut oil

1 red bell pepper, seeded and diced

1 (14-ounce) can coconut milk

3 tablespoons red Thai curry paste

1. **Preheat the oven and prepare a baking sheet.** Preheat the oven to 400°F. Line a baking sheet with aluminum foil and coat with cooking spray. Set aside.

2. **Prepare the meatballs.** In a medium bowl, combine the ground pork, bread crumbs, garlic, ginger, curry powder, salt, and half the onion (reserve the other half for the sauce). Mix well. Form the pork mixture into meatballs (about 2 tablespoons each) and place on the prepared sheet pan.

3. **Bake.** Bake the meatballs for 20 minutes.

4. **Prepare the sauce.** While the meatballs bake, heat the coconut oil in a large skillet over medium-high heat. Add the reserved onion and the pepper and cook for about 5 minutes, or until softened. Stir in the coconut milk and curry paste.

5. **Cook the sauce.** Turn the heat to low and bring the sauce to a simmer. Cook for about 10 minutes, or until the meatballs are finished baking.

6. **Add the meatballs to the sauce.** Add the baked meatballs to the sauce and ladle the sauce over them to cover. Cook for 2 to 3 minutes, or until heated through.

7. **Finish.** Serve the meatballs and sauce over rice, cauliflower rice, or zucchini noodles, as desired, and garnish with the cilantro.

Make It Gluten Free: Use almond meal instead of bread crumbs.

Per Serving: Calories: 667; Saturated Fat: 18g; Total Fat: 48g; Protein: 22g; Total Carbs: 27g; Fiber: 1g; Sodium: 3,971mg

ONE-PAN ITALIAN SAUSAGE AND VEGETABLES

SERVES: 4 | PREP TIME: 10 minutes COOK TIME: 20 minutes |

Smoked paprika is one of my favorite "secret" ingredients; it really adds that special something to this dish. This one-pan meal is filling as-is, but feel free to add a side of rice or quinoa to round it out.

1 pound Brussels sprouts, quartered

8 ounces green beans, trimmed and cut into 2-inch pieces

1 red onion, cut into 1-inch pieces

1 red bell pepper, seeded and cut into 1-inch pieces

¼ cup olive oil

3 garlic cloves, minced

1 teaspoon smoked paprika

½ teaspoon salt

½ teaspoon freshly ground black pepper

1 pound Italian sausage links

1. **Preheat the oven.** Preheat the oven to 425°F.

2. **Prepare the sausage and vegetables.** On a baking sheet, combine the Brussels sprouts, green beans, onion, pepper, oil, garlic, paprika, salt, and pepper. Stir well to combine.

3. **Add the sausage.** Place the sausages on top of the vegetable mixture.

4. **Finish.** Bake for 20 minutes, or until the vegetables are tender and the sausage is golden brown and cooked through.

Make It Faster: Shred the Brussels sprouts and cut the Italian sausage into pieces to reduce the cooking time by 5 minutes.

Smart Shopping: Look for shredded Brussels sprouts at your grocery store.

Per Serving: Calories: 369; Saturated Fat: 6g; Total Fat: 23g; Protein: 24g; Total Carbs: 23g; Fiber: 8g; Sodium: 970mg

GRILLED STEAK WITH CILANTRO AVOCADO SAUCE

SERVES: 4 to 6 | PREP TIME: 15 minutes COOK TIME: 10 minutes

I'm all about sauces, and this cilantro avocado sauce is no exception. The flavors of cilantro, lime, and garlic shine through this fresh and zippy sauce, and it pairs perfectly with the chili powder and cumin–spiced steaks. I love grilling flank steaks, but really any cut of beef you like will do! I serve these steaks with grilled corn on the cob—it's so easy, and I love the grilled flavor on the corn!

For the cilantro avocado sauce

1 avocado, halved and pitted
2 tablespoons olive oil
⅓ cup fresh cilantro
Juice of 1 lime
1 garlic clove, peeled
½ teaspoon salt

For the grilled steak and corn

1 tablespoon butter, melted
1 teaspoon chili powder
½ teaspoon garlic powder
½ teaspoon ground cumin
1½ to 2 pounds sirloin or flank steak
Salt
Freshly ground black pepper
4 to 6 ears corn, husked
2 tablespoons olive oil

1. **Prepare the sauce.** Scoop the avocado flesh into a food processor and add the oil, cilantro, lime juice, garlic, and salt. Blend until smooth. Set aside.

2. **Preheat the grill.** Preheat the grill to medium-high heat.

3. **Prepare the steaks.** In a small bowl, whisk the melted butter, chili powder, garlic powder, and cumin until combined. Brush each steak with the butter mixture and season with salt and pepper.

4. **Prepare the corn.** Brush the corn with the oil and season with salt and pepper.

5. **Grill the steaks and corn.** Place the corn directly on the grill and cook for about 2 minutes, turn 3 or 4 times while cooking. At the same time, place the steaks on the grill and cook for 4 to 5 minutes per side for medium to medium-well steaks, 155°F to 160°F on an instant-read thermometer.

6. **Finish.** Serve the steaks topped with the cilantro avocado sauce.

Love Your Leftovers: If you have any leftover steak, use it on a salad for lunch the next day.

Per Serving: Calories: 589; Saturated Fat: 9g; Total Fat: 35g; Protein: 54g; Total Carbs: 20g; Fiber: 5g; Sodium: 464mg

ITALIAN SLOPPY JOES

SERVES: 4 | **PREP TIME:** 10 minutes **COOK TIME:** 20 minutes

Sloppy joes were part of the dinner rotation when I was growing up, and I never had a desire to make them as an adult. However, I will make an exception for these. Instead of a regular bun, they are open-faced, made with buttered Texas toast, and topped with mozzarella. These are not your mom's sloppy joes.

For the Texas toast

8 slices Texas toast bread
4 tablespoons butter, at room temperature
Garlic salt, for seasoning

For the sloppy joes

1 pound ground beef
1 small white onion, diced
1½ cups marinara sauce
1 cup shredded mozza-rella cheese

1. **Preheat the oven.** Preheat the oven to 425°F.

2. **Prepare the toast.** Spread 1½ teaspoons of butter on each slice. Sprinkle with the garlic salt.

3. **Bake the toast.** Place the toast on a baking sheet and bake for 8 minutes, flipping halfway through the baking time. Remove and leave the oven on.

4. **Prepare the sloppy joe mixture.** In a large skillet over medium-high heat, cook the ground beef for 5 to 7 minutes, or until browned, breaking it up with the back of a wooden spoon as it cooks, until it is no longer pink.

5. **Add the onion.** Add the onion and cook for 5 minutes, or until it is softened.

6. **Add the marinara.** Stir in the marinara and cook for 3 to 4 minutes, or until warmed through.

7. **Top the Texas toast.** Evenly distribute the sloppy joe mixture over each slice of toast and top with mozzarella.

8. **Finish.** Bake for 2 to 3 minutes, or until the cheese melts.

Make It Faster: Use frozen Texas toast that is already buttered and seasoned. Simply bake it according to the package directions, top it with the sloppy joe mixture and cheese, and melt the cheese.

Make It Healthier: Feel free to use the sloppy joe mixture on top of zucchini noodles or whole wheat buns instead of Texas toast!

Per Serving: Calories: 571; Saturated Fat: 14g; Total Fat: 27g; Protein: 37g; Total Carbs: 49g; Fiber: 4g; Sodium: 1,229mg

CHIPOTLE BEEF TACO PASTA

SERVES: 6 | PREP TIME: 5 minutes COOK TIME: 20 minutes |

This cheesy pasta dish is perfect for that time of year when you crave comfort food but don't want to wait hours for it to cook. Chipotle peppers in adobo sauce add a fun smoky, spicy flavor to this one-pot pasta. If you have little ones who don't like spicy foods, just omit the chipotle peppers, and it will be entirely family-friendly!

1 pound ground beef

3 cups dry macaroni or rotini pasta

2 cups beef broth

1 cup prepared salsa

¼ cup water

1 (1-ounce) package taco seasoning

2 tablespoons finely diced chipotle peppers in adobo sauce

1½ cups shredded Cheddar cheese

½ cup sour cream

Diced tomatoes, for topping

Chopped scallions, for topping

1. **Cook the beef.** In a large skillet over medium-high heat, cook the ground beef for 5 minutes, breaking it up with the back of a wooden spoon into small pieces as it cooks, until it is no longer pink. Drain the fat from the skillet.

2. **Add the pasta and seasoning.** Stir in the pasta, broth, salsa, water, taco seasoning, and chipotle. Bring the mixture to a boil, reduce the heat to medium, and cover the skillet.

3. **Cook the pasta.** Cook the mixture for 12 to 15 minutes, or until the pasta absorbs the liquid and is tender.

4. **Add the sour cream and cheese.** Stir in the cheese and sour cream and cook until well combined.

5. **Finish.** Serve topped with tomatoes and scallions.

Make It Healthier: To lighten this dish, use plain Greek yogurt instead of sour cream.

Make It Yourself: If you have time, make your own Taco Seasoning (use 2 tablespoons in this recipe; page 136).

Per Serving: Calories: 490; Saturated Fat: 11g; Total Fat: 20g; Protein: 32g; Total Carbs: 45g; Fiber: 3g; Sodium: 822mg

THAI BASIL BEEF AND NOODLES

SERVES: 4 to 6 | PREP TIME: 10 minutes COOK TIME: 15 minutes

Thinly sliced pieces of steak, green beans, Thai basil, and saucy noodles . . . who needs takeout? This staple recipe is tasty, healthy, and affordable, because you're making it at home. I really love using wide rice noodles in this dish, as there seems to be more surface area to soak up the flavorful sauce. Thai basil has a more savory and licorice-like flavor that really complements the beef in this dish, but Italian basil can definitely be used instead if you don't have Thai basil.

For the sauce

⅓ cup soy sauce

2 garlic cloves, minced

2 teaspoons minced peeled fresh ginger

2 tablespoons water

1 tablespoon honey

¼ to ½ teaspoon red pepper flakes

For the Thai basil beef and noodles

8 ounces wide rice noodles

2 tablespoons canola oil, divided

1 pound sirloin steak, thinly sliced against the grain

1 red onion, thinly sliced

2 cups cut (2-inch pieces) green beans

¼ cup fresh Thai basil

1. **Prepare the sauce.** In a small bowl, whisk the soy sauce, garlic, ginger, water, honey, and red pepper flakes until combined. Set aside.

2. **Cook the noodles.** In a large bowl, combine the rice noodles and enough hot water to cover. Let soak for about 10 minutes, or until just tender. Drain the noodles and rinse with cold water.

3. **Cook the beef.** While the noodles soak, heat 1 tablespoon of oil in a large skillet or wok over medium-high heat. Add the beef and cook for about 5 minutes, or until golden. Remove the beef from the skillet and set aside.

4. **Cook the onion and green beans.** Return the skillet to the heat and add the remaining 1 tablespoon of oil, the onion, and the green beans. Cook for about 5 minutes, or until the vegetables are softened.

5. **Add the sauce, beef, and noodles to the skillet.** Return the beef to the skillet and stir in the sauce. Add the noodles to the skillet and toss to combine. Let the mixture come to a simmer.

6. **Finish.** Serve topped with the basil.

Love Your Leftovers: Add a splash of soy sauce to leftover noodles to make up for the sauce that the noodles absorbed.

Per Serving: Calories: 568; Saturated Fat: 7g; Total Fat: 24g; Protein: 27g; Total Carbs: 61g; Fiber: 4g; Sodium: 1,362mg

TACO STUFFED PEPPERS

SERVES: 4 | PREP TIME: 10 minutes COOK TIME: 20 minutes

Sometimes there's nothing better than a straight-up taco, but taco night takes all forms in our house—taco pasta, taco salads, taco stuffed peppers. It all qualifies for Taco Tuesday in my book. As a bonus, these Taco Stuffed Peppers are a healthier, veggie-filled option, and using your homemade taco seasoning also makes these gluten-free. The peppers are parcooked in the microwave to reduce the overall cooking time, and this trick works like a charm. Don't forget the toppings—these stuffed peppers are begging to be topped with guacamole and sour cream!

4 large bell peppers,
  any color, tops cut off
  and seeded
1 pound ground beef
1 white onion, diced
1 red bell pepper, seeded
  and diced
2 tablespoons store-bought
  taco seasoning
1 cup shredded Monterey
  Jack cheese
Shredded lettuce,
  for topping
Guacamole, for topping
Sour cream, for topping

1. **Preheat the oven.** Preheat the oven to 425°F.

2. **Parcook the peppers.** Place the whole peppers on a microwave-safe plate, cover with a damp paper towel, and microwave on high power for 4 minutes, or until tender.

3. **Cook the ground beef.** While the peppers cook, cook the ground beef for about 5 minutes in a large skillet over medium-high heat until browned, breaking it up into small pieces with the back of a wooden spoon as it cooks.

4. **Cook the vegetables.** Add the onion and diced pepper and cook for 5 minutes.

5. **Add the taco seasoning.** Stir in the taco seasoning.

6. **Assemble.** Evenly distribute the beef mixture among the peppers and top with the cheese.

7. **Bake.** Bake for 5 to 8 minutes, or until the cheese melts.

8. **Finish.** Top with the lettuce, guacamole, and sour cream.

Make It Yourself: If you have extra time, make your own Taco Seasoning Mix (page 136).

Per Serving: Calories: 474; Saturated Fat: 13g; Total Fat: 27g; Protein: 33g; Total Carbs: 27g; Fiber: 4g; Sodium: 974mg

CHAPTER NINE
BASICS AND STAPLES

Although all the recipes in this cookbook can be made in 30 minutes or less, there are some parts that you can take a little more time with, if you have it. I love making things from scratch, such as Taco Seasoning Mix (page 136) and Teriyaki Sauce (page 138), as I know the ingredients are not processed and are much healthier for my family and me. Other recipes, such as the Italian Meatballs (page 142) and Perfect Whole Roasted Chicken (page 144), can be made ahead of time for future use, making weeknight cooking even faster!

CURRY POWDER

Makes about ¾ cup | **PREP TIME:** 10 minutes | 🕐

It never occurred to me to make my own curry powder until I realized I had run out when cooking dinner one night. After a quick Google search, I found out that it's easy and SO worth it to make your own! I like to buy my spices in bulk from our local co-op, as they are cheaper that way. Curry powder is called for in my Chickpea and Kale Curry (page 73) and Thai Coconut Curry Meatballs (page 125).

3 tablespoons ground coriander

3 tablespoons ground cumin

2 tablespoons ground turmeric

2 tablespoons ground ginger

1 tablespoon dry mustard

1 tablespoon freshly ground black pepper

1 tablespoon ground cinnamon

1 teaspoon ground cardamom

½ teaspoon cayenne pepper

1. **Prepare the curry powder.** In an airtight container, stir together the coriander, cumin, turmeric, ginger, mustard, black pepper, cinnamon, cardamom, and cayenne.

2. **Store.** Cover and store for up to 3 years.

Make It Spicier: If you like your food on the spicier side, add ¼ to ½ teaspoon more cayenne.

Per Serving (1 tablespoon): Calories: 21; Saturated Fat: 0g; Total Fat: 1g; Protein: 1g; Total Carbs: 3g; Fiber: 1g; Sodium: 4mg

TACO SEASONING MIX

Makes about ⅓ cup | **PREP TIME:** 10 minutes | 🕐

We are big taco eaters in our family, so it's important to me that our taco seasoning is as fresh and healthy as possible. This homemade taco seasoning is preservative-free and doesn't have anything artificial in it. It's a versatile blend that can be used in tacos, burritos, pastas, or salad dressings! I use taco seasoning mix in my Chipotle Beef Taco Pasta (page 129) and Taco Stuffed Peppers (page 131).

¼ cup chili powder

2 tablespoons ground cumin

2 teaspoons salt

1 teaspoon dried oregano

1 teaspoon onion powder

1 teaspoon paprika

1 teaspoon garlic powder

½ teaspoon freshly ground black pepper

¼ to ½ teaspoon cayenne pepper, to taste

1. **Prepare the mix.** In a small bowl, combine the chili powder, cumin, salt, oregano, onion powder, paprika, garlic powder, black pepper, and cayenne. Whisk well to blend.

2. **Store.** Store the seasoning in an airtight container for up to 3 years.

Per Serving (1 tablespoon): Calories: 30; Saturated Fat: 0g; Total Fat: 1g; Protein: 1g; Total Carbs: 5g; Fiber: 2g; Sodium: 832mg

PESTO

Makes 1 cup | **PREP TIME:** 10 minutes | ⏰

Pesto is one of the most versatile sauces for everyday cooking. You can use pesto as a marinade, a sandwich spread, as a pasta sauce, or even just as a dip. If it's the middle of summer and you happen to have a bounty of fresh basil, double this recipe and freeze what you don't immediately use! You'll be happy you did when winter blows in. For ideas, see my Pesto Turkey Burgers (page 49) or Creamy Chicken Sausage Pesto Pasta (page 101).

2 cups fresh basil

¼ cup shredded Parmesan cheese

¼ cup pine nuts

3 garlic cloves, peeled

½ teaspoon salt

½ teaspoon freshly ground black pepper

½ cup olive oil

1. **Prepare the pesto base.** In a food processor, combine the basil, cheese, pine nuts, garlic, salt, and pepper. Pulse until the mixture resembles coarse crumbs.

2. **Add the olive oil.** With the food processor running, slowly add the olive oil. Process for 30 to 60 seconds.

3. **Store.** Refrigerate in an airtight container for up to 1 week, or freeze for up to 6 months.

Per Serving (2 tablespoons): Calories: 151; Saturated Fat: 3g; Total Fat: 16g; Protein: 2g; Total Carbs: 1g; Fiber: 0g; Sodium: 180mg

TERIYAKI SAUCE

Makes 1½ cups | PREP TIME: 5 minutes COOK TIME: 8 minutes

This homemade teriyaki sauce is such a lifesaver when I want to make a quick stir-fry. This sauce is made with ingredients I always have on hand, and without any funky ingredients that might be found in the store-bought versions. Try this homemade teriyaki sauce in my Chicken Teriyaki Wraps (page 52) or the Teriyaki Pork and Pineapple Stir-Fry (page 121)!

1 cup plus 2 tablespoons
   water, divided
⅓ cup soy sauce
2 tablespoons light
   brown sugar
1 tablespoon honey
1 tablespoon apple
   cider vinegar
3 garlic cloves, minced
½ teaspoon ground ginger
2 tablespoons cornstarch

1. **Boil.** In a small pot over medium heat, combine 1 cup of water, the soy sauce, brown sugar, honey, vinegar, garlic, and ginger. Bring to a boil and cook for 1 minute.

2. **Thicken the sauce.** In a small bowl, whisk the cornstarch with the remaining 2 tablespoons of water until the cornstarch dissolves. Add the cornstarch slurry to the pot and cook for 5 minutes more, or until the sauce has thickened.

3. **Store.** Refrigerate in an airtight container for up to 1 week, or freeze for up to 4 months.

Per Serving (1 tablespoon): Calories: 11; Saturated Fat: 0g;
Total Fat: 0g; Protein: 0g; Total Carbs: 3g; Fiber: 0g; Sodium: 200mg

PANCAKE MIX

Makes about 4½ cups (1 cup makes 6 pancakes) | PREP TIME: 10 minutes
COOK TIME: 10 minutes

Mornings with pancakes are always a fun surprise for my boys, and this pancake mix makes it a breeze to whip them up. I make a big batch, so whenever the craving strikes I have a homemade mix waiting for me. I also love using this mix in my Mixed Berry Pancake Muffins (page 23).

For the pancake mix

4 cups all-purpose flour

3 tablespoons baking powder

3 tablespoons sugar

2 teaspoons baking soda

1 teaspoon salt

1 teaspoon ground cinnamon (optional)

For the batter (per 1 cup of dry mix)

1 cup pancake mix

1 large egg

1 cup milk

1 tablespoon melted butter

1. **Prepare the pancake mix.** In a large resealable plastic bag, combine the flour, baking powder, sugar, baking soda, salt, and cinnamon (if using). Seal the bag and shake well to combine.

2. **Prepare the batter.** In a medium bowl, stir together 1 cup of pancake mix, the egg, milk, and melted butter until just combined.

3. **Preheat the griddle.** Preheat a griddle or skillet over medium-high heat.

4. **Cook the pancakes.** Pour about ¼ cup of pancake batter onto the warm griddle. Cook for 3 to 4 minutes, or until bubbles form on the surface. Flip and cook for 2 to 3 minutes more.

5. **Store.** Refrigerate any leftover batter in an airtight container for up to 2 days and dry mix for up to 6 months.

Make It Faster: You can make these pancakes ahead of time. Prepared pancakes can be refrigerated in an airtight container for up to five days, or frozen for two months.

Per Serving (3 pancakes): Calories: 395; Saturated Fat: 6g;
Total Fat: 12g; Protein: 14g; Total Carbs: 60g; Fiber: 8g; Sodium: 668mg

PAN-SAUTÉED VEGETABLES

SERVES: 4 to 6 | **PREP TIME:** 10 minutes **COOK TIME:** 12 minutes

This is my go-to side dish when I have a protein and a grain and just need some vegetables to round the meal out. It is completely adaptable to any vegetables you might have lurking in your veggie drawer. Just chop, sauté, and season! Many of the protein dishes in this book would pair well with a side of these freshly sautéed vegetables, and I've included different seasoning suggestions to match accordingly.

2 tablespoons olive oil

1 zucchini, sliced

1 summer squash, sliced

1 red onion, sliced

8 ounces mushrooms, sliced

2 garlic cloves, minced

½ teaspoon salt

½ teaspoon freshly ground black pepper

Italian

1 teaspoon Italian seasoning

Indian

1 teaspoon Curry Powder (page 135)

Mexican

1 teaspoon Taco Seasoning Mix (page 136)

1. **Prepare the pan.** In a large skillet over medium-high heat, heat the oil.

2. **Cook the vegetables.** Add the zucchini, squash, onion, and mushrooms to the skillet and cook for about 10 minutes, or until the vegetables are softened. I like to cover the pan to also steam them and speed up the cooking process a bit.

3. **Season.** Add the garlic, salt, and pepper, and any additional spices you like. Cook for another minute.

4. **Store.** Refrigerate in an airtight container for up to 2 days.

Per Serving: Calories: 102; Saturated Fat: 1g; Total Fat: 7g; Protein: 3g; Total Carbs: 8g; Fiber: 2g; Sodium: 305mg

ROASTED RED PEPPERS

Makes 4 roasted peppers | PREP TIME: 5 minutes
COOK TIME: 35 minutes, plus 20 minutes to steam

Roasted red peppers are super handy for quick, healthy meals. They're simple to make and add a ton of flavor to any recipe. I use roasted red peppers in a number of recipes in this cookbook and, although using the jarred version is convenient and saves on time, making them at home definitely saves a bit of money. If you're looking for ideas, check out my Roasted Red Pepper Gazpacho (page 38), Gruyère and Roasted Red Pepper Tuna Melts (page 51), or Roasted Red Pepper and Goat Cheese Egg Muffins (page 22).

4 red bell peppers
2 tablespoons olive oil

1. **Preheat the oven.** Preheat the oven to 425°F.

2. **Prepare the peppers.** Place the peppers on a baking sheet and brush with the olive oil.

3. **Roast the peppers.** Roast the peppers for 20 minutes. Flip them and roast for 15 minutes more.

4. **Steam the peppers.** Remove the baking sheet from the oven and cover it with aluminum foil. Let the peppers steam for 20 minutes.

5. **Remove the seeds and peel.** Remove the foil. Cut the stems off the peppers and remove the seeds. Peel the peppers—the skins should slide right off.

6. **Slice.** Slice the peeled peppers into strips, or dice them, depending on how you are using them.

7. **Store.** Refrigerator in an airtight container for up to 1 week, or freeze for up to 4 months.

Technique Trick: If parts of the peel do not slide off easily, simply use a knife or a vegetable peeler to cut them off.

Per Serving: Calories: 98; Saturated Fat: 1g; Total Fat: 7g; Protein: 1g; Total Carbs: 9g; Fiber: 2g; Sodium: 3mg

ITALIAN MEATBALLS

Makes about 24 meatballs | PREP TIME: 10 minutes COOK TIME: 20 minutes

Meatballs taste just fine when bought at the store but taste AMAZING when you make them yourself. They might take an extra half hour, but, man, the wait is worth it! I love making a batch and freezing them for whenever I need them. Of course you can use them in spaghetti and meatballs, but we are big fans of meatball subs and meatball soup, too!

Nonstick cooking spray
1 pound ground beef
8 ounces ground pork
1 cup Italian bread crumbs
½ cup milk
2 large eggs
¼ cup grated Parmesan cheese
2 tablespoons roughly chopped fresh parsley
1 tablespoon Worcestershire sauce
1 teaspoon kosher salt

1. **Preheat the oven and prepare a baking sheet.** Preheat the oven to 375°F. Line a baking sheet with aluminum foil and coat with cooking spray.

2. **Mix the meatball ingredients.** In a large bowl, combine the ground beef, ground pork, bread crumbs, milk, eggs, cheese, parsley, Worcestershire sauce, and salt. Using a spatula or your hands, mix the ingredients until just combined. Be careful not to overmix.

3. **Form the meatballs.** Scoop out 2 tablespoons of the meat mixture and form it into a ball. Place on the prepared baking sheet and repeat until you have about 24 meatballs.

4. **Cook the meatballs.** Bake for 18 to 20 minutes, or until the meatballs are cooked through and reach an internal temperature of 165°F on an instant-read thermometer.

5. **Store.** Refrigerate in an airtight container for up to 4 days, or freeze for up to 3 months.

Per Serving (4 meatballs): Calories: 324; Saturated Fat: 6g; Total Fat: 16g; Protein: 29g; Total Carbs: 16g; Fiber: 1g; Sodium: 886mg

EASY TOMATO PASTA SAUCE

Makes 2 cups | PREP TIME: 10 minutes COOK TIME: 55 minutes

There are a lot of great options for store-bought tomato sauces these days, but when the farmers' market is bursting with fresh tomatoes, I can't help but whip up a few batches of my own. My "secret" ingredient for my pasta sauce is butter—it adds a richness that is worth the extra effort of making your own sauce. I freeze any leftover sauce to use during those dark winter months when I'm craving fresh summer flavors. You can use this sauce in Eggplant Parmesan Sandwiches (page 61) and Italian Sloppy Joes (page 128).

2 tablespoons olive oil

1 white onion, sliced

4 garlic cloves, minced

2 pounds (about 6 large) tomatoes, peeled, cored, and cut into ½-inch chunks

2 tablespoons salted butter

2 tablespoons tomato paste

Salt

Freshly ground black pepper

1. **Cook the onions.** In a large pot over medium heat, heat the olive oil. Add the onion and cook for 5 to 7 minutes, or until softened.

2. **Cook the garlic.** Add the garlic and cook for 1 minute.

3. **Cook the tomatoes.** Add the tomatoes, butter, and tomato paste and stir well to combine. Turn the heat to medium-low and cook the sauce for 40 to 45 minutes, stirring every 10 minutes. Season with salt and pepper.

4. **Store.** Refrigerate in an airtight container for up to 1 week, or freeze for up to 4 months.

Per Serving (½ cup): Calories: 174; Saturated Fat: 5g; Total Fat: 13g; Protein: 3g; Total Carbs: 14g; Fiber: 4g; Sodium: 100mg

PERFECT WHOLE ROASTED CHICKEN

SERVES: 6 | **PREP TIME:** 10 minutes **COOK TIME:** 1 hour, 10 minutes

Roasting a chicken is my all-time favorite thing to do to make me feel like a real cook. Not only is it delicious and versatile, but it's economical, too! I am a big fan of using the bones to make bone broth after I remove all the meat from them, to use as much of the chicken as possible. The meat is great for adding to salads or making sandwiches, casseroles, and soups throughout the week—or in dishes like my Creamy Chicken Sausage Pesto Pasta (page 101) and Korean Barbecue Chicken Tacos (page 54).

1 (4- to 5-pound) whole chicken

2 tablespoons butter, melted

1 tablespoon chopped fresh rosemary leaves

1 teaspoon kosher salt

½ teaspoon freshly ground black pepper

1. **Preheat the oven.** Preheat the oven to 425°F.

2. **Prepare the chicken.** Place the chicken in a roasting pan and pat it dry with a paper towel. Brush the chicken with the butter and sprinkle with the rosemary, salt, and pepper.

3. **Bake the chicken.** Bake for 60 to 70 minutes, or until the internal temperature in the breast reaches 165°F on an instant-read thermometer. Let rest for 5 minutes before slicing and serving.

4. **Store.** Refrigerate the chicken in an airtight container for up to 4 days, or freeze for up to 3 months.

Per Serving: Calories: 240; Saturated Fat: 6g; Total Fat: 15g; Protein: 23g; Total Carbs: 2g; Fiber: 0g; Sodium: 526mg

The Dirty Dozen™ and the Clean Fifteen™

A nonprofit environmental watchdog organization called Environmental Working Group (EWG) looks at data supplied by the US Department of Agriculture (USDA) and the Food and Drug Administration (FDA) about pesticide residues. Each year it compiles a list of the best and worst pesticide loads found in commercial crops. You can use these lists to decide which fruits and vegetables to buy organic to minimize your exposure to pesticides and which produce is considered safe enough to buy conventionally. This does not mean they are pesticide-free, though, so wash these fruits and vegetables thoroughly. The list is updated annually, and you can find it online at EWG.org/FoodNews.

DIRTY DOZEN™

1. strawberries
2. spinach
3. kale
4. nectarines
5. apples
6. grapes
7. peaches
8. cherries
9. pears
10. tomatoes
11. celery
12. potatoes

Additionally, nearly three-quarters of hot pepper samples contained pesticide residues.

CLEAN FIFTEEN™

1. avocados
2. sweet corn*
3. pineapples
4. sweet peas (frozen)
5. onions
6. papayas*
7. eggplants
8. asparagus
9. kiwis
10. cabbages
11. cauliflower
12. cantaloupes
13. broccoli
14. mushrooms
15. honeydew melons

* A small amount of sweet corn, papaya, and summer squash sold in the United States is produced from genetically modified seeds. Buy organic varieties of these crops if you want to avoid genetically modified produce.

146

Measurement Conversions

	US STANDARD	US STANDARD (OUNCES)	METRIC (APPROXIMATE)
VOLUME EQUIVALENTS (LIQUID)	2 tablespoons	1 fl. oz.	30 mL
	¼ cup	2 fl. oz.	60 mL
	½ cup	4 fl. oz.	120 mL
	1 cup	8 fl. oz.	240 mL
	1½ cups	12 fl. oz.	355 mL
	2 cups or 1 pint	16 fl. oz.	475 mL
	4 cups or 1 quart	32 fl. oz.	1 L
	1 gallon	128 fl. oz.	4 L
VOLUME EQUIVALENTS (DRY)	⅛ teaspoon	———	0.5 mL
	¼ teaspoon	———	1 mL
	½ teaspoon	———	2 mL
	¾ teaspoon	———	4 mL
	1 teaspoon	———	5 mL
	1 tablespoon	———	15 mL
	¼ cup	———	59 mL
	⅓ cup	———	79 mL
	½ cup	———	118 mL
	⅔ cup	———	156 mL
	¾ cup	———	177 mL
	1 cup	———	235 mL
	2 cups or 1 pint	———	475 mL
	3 cups	———	700 mL
	4 cups or 1 quart	———	1 L
	½ gallon	———	2 L
	1 gallon	———	4 L
WEIGHT EQUIVALENTS	½ ounce	———	15 g
	1 ounce	———	30 g
	2 ounces	———	60 g
	4 ounces	———	115 g
	8 ounces	———	225 g
	12 ounces	———	340 g
	16 ounces or 1 pound	———	455 g

	FAHRENHEIT (F)	CELSIUS (C) (APPROXIMATE)
OVEN TEMPERATURES	250°F	120°F
	300°F	150°C
	325°F	180°C
	375°F	190°C
	400°F	200°C
	425°F	220°C
	450°F	230°C

Recipe Index

Index

Acknowledgments

Thank you to my husband, Marc, for always supporting me and encouraging me to go after my dreams, no matter how challenging or risky.

To my parents, who taught me unconditional love and to never settle for average.

To all of my friends and family who have supported and encouraged me along the way—you all are truly the best!

About the Author

Taylor Ellingson is a self-taught baker and home cook who loves creating healthy meals and decadent desserts. Even more, she loves introducing people to cooking and showing them how easy it can be! She is the founder of the food blog Greens & Chocolate (www.greensnchocolate.com), where she writes mostly about her recipe creations and occasionally about her family life and travel adventures. When she's not cooking and eating, she enjoys running, yoga, hiking, travel, patio happy hours, and spending time with her family. She was born and raised in Iowa and currently lives in Minneapolis, Minnesota, with her husband, Marc, and their two boys, Lars and Soren.